Understanding

LAND CONTRACT HOMES

In Pursuit of the American Dream

∂∞∾

Michael ·Delaware

If, And or But
Publishing Company

Published by
'If, And or But' Publishing Company
P.O. Box 2559
Battle Creek, Michigan 49016 USA
www.ifandorbutpublishing.com

ISBN-13: 978-0615923352 (If, And or But Publishing)
ISBN-10: 0615923356

This book also contains clipart illustrations which were acquired by means of royalty free usage rights in 2013 and are copyright to: GraphicsFactory.com on pages: 1,7,9,14,17,24,25,44 & 107. All other illustrations are copyright to *If, And or But Publishing.*

While attempts have been made to verify all information provided in this publication; neither the author nor the publisher assumes any responsibility for errors, omissions, or contrary interpretations of the subject matter herein. The views expressed are those of the author alone, and should not be taken as expert instruction or commands.

This book is sold with the understanding that neither the author nor the publisher is engaged in rendering legal, accounting, or other professional advice. If legal or other expert assistance is required, the services of a competent person should be sought.

In Memory of
Marguerite Hill

Table of Contents

Introduction

❧

Before proceeding, it is important to make a necessary disclaimer concerning legal advice. None of the information contained in this book is intended to constitute legal or other professional advice. You should not rely solely on the information contained in this book for making legal decisions. It is recommended one consult with an attorney or other professionals for specific advice tailored to your situation in the area of which you are doing business.

The information contained herein has been obtained through sources deemed reliable but cannot be guaranteed as to its accuracy. Any information of special interest should be obtained through independent verification.

This book was prepared and compiled to help educate the reader on the subject of seller financing. Land Contracts as will be explained in detail in this book is a form of seller financing wherein the buyer secures the home with a down payment, and makes monthly payments inclusive of both interest and principle to the seller over a period of time and stipulates that the buyer will settle the balance in full at a future date.

I use the term 'Land Contract' as the main descriptive term for this type of seller financing throughout this book, as it is the most commonly known in the area of the Midwest U.S. where I reside. However, seller financing known as a 'Land Contract' is also commonly known as 'Contract for Deed', 'Trust Deeds', 'Deeds of Trust', 'Notes', 'Private Money Mortgages', 'Privately Held Mortgages' and 'Seller Financed Mortgages' depending on what market or region you are in the country.

Some may have slight variations in how they are executed within each State, but all essentially fall under the broad brushstroke description of 'Seller Financing'. For simplicity I use the term 'Land Contract' as the descriptive term throughout this book. In this new addition of this book, I am also including an expanded resources page at the end where you may check out further information on this subject.

Much of the information in this book was compiled from several blog articles that I wrote between 2009 and 2012 on the subject of seller financing and land contracts. Please forgive me if at times in going through this material that the chapters flow differently at times, as the book was edited to attempt to keep much of the original information intact. I have attempted to organize it without losing the importance of some of the technical material contained herein.

You will find as you read this book that I neither encourage nor try to discourage the option to purchase or sell by means of a Land Contract. This information is provided here so that you can gain an understanding of the subject, and its use as a possible tool to facilitate the acquisition of property.

I formulated the original idea to write this book on Land Contracts when I found in the course of doing business that there was so much interest in the subject, and at the same time so much misinformation. The motivation and driving pursuit of homeownership compels one to seek all avenues, and the method of the Land Contract can make the otherwise complex process of attaining that goal seem simple.

This drive for a more simple and fast means to acquire the dream of homeownership has made Land Contracts somewhat of an 'Urban Legend' among would-be buyers. An 'Urban Legend' could best be defined as: 'A secondhand story or folklore told as true and just plausible enough to be believed, but not entirely based on fact.'

In this book I have sought to remove the blanket of misunderstanding and bring clarity to the subject for all who are interested, and at the same time re-kindle the fire of the American Dream.

Such is the scope of this book. I hope to not only inform the reader on the subject of seller financing and its use, but also to provide other options for cases where an alternative approach may seem more practical. Land Contracts are a means to achieve homeownership, and used correctly are an excellent way to go when conditions are right and the subject is well understood.

If you have further interest in this subject as an investor, I have also written a companion book to this one entitled: Land Contract Homes for Investors.

Chapter One

Origins in the Pursuit of Happiness

છ્જ

In a book dedicated to exploring the subject of seller financing, it is interesting to note that it has deep roots in the founding of the United States, and even derives some of its origins from English law. Early drafts of the 'Declaration of Independence' used the phrase 'Life, Liberty and the Pursuit of Property' and were later modified to what we know today in the full paragraph as:

"We hold these truths to be self-evident, that all men are created equal, that they are endowed by their creator with certain inalienable Rights that among these are Life, Liberty and the pursuit of Happiness."

These timeless words were written by Thomas Jefferson in 1776 in the famous 'Declaration of Independence'. The precise origin of the inspiration or influence of the ideal expressed as the 'Pursuit of Happiness' has been debated by historians and scholars for a very long time. In one popular hypothesis it is said to derive from 17th Century English philosopher John Locke, regarded as the 'enlightenment thinker' of his day.

Locke wrote a publication in 1689 entitled 'The Two Treatises on Government' in which he claimed that civil society was created for the protection of property. In this treatise, he expressed this ideal with the phrase "Life, Liberty and Estate" maintaining that political society was created for the better protection of property.

As an alternative hypothesis, another 17th century English philosopher named Richard Cumberland is also cited as a source for having written that "promoting the well-being of our fellow humans is essential to the pursuit of our own happiness."

The phrase is also said to derive from an English translation of Swiss Legal and Political Theorist Jean Jacques Burlamaqui's Principles of Natural and Politic Law treatise prepared in 1763 where he described the "noble pursuit" of "true and solid happiness" in the opening chapter discussing 'natural rights' of a society.

Perhaps Jefferson's inspirations were his fellow colonialists. In 1774 the First Continental Congress was formed among the American Colonies following the British Parliament passing what came to be known as the 'Intolerable Acts'. The 'Intolerable Acts' were a series of laws passed by the British in the wake of the Boston Tea Party. These laws in the view of the colonials were a direct violation of their own rights and freedoms, and fueled the growth of the American Revolution.

The independent colonies sent representatives to a meeting in Philadelphia and together they jointly composed and ratified a detailed bill of rights on October 14, 1774 which came to be known as the 'Declaration of Colonial Rights' in which they expressed among their grievances the following: "That they are entitled to life, liberty and property: and they have never ceded to any foreign power whatever, a right to dispose of either without their consent."

Further, in June of 1776, the Virginia Convention of Delegates met, drafted and passed the Virginia Declaration of Rights for their colony written by George Mason, which stated: "That all men are by nature equally free and independent, and have certain inherent rights, of which, when they enter into a state of society, they cannot, by any compact, deprive or divest their posterity; namely, the enjoyment of life and liberty, with the means of acquiring and possessing property, and pursuing and obtaining happiness and safety."

Thomas Jefferson himself was from Virginia, and arrived at the Second Continental Congress with the Virginia Delegation. It could therefore be concluded that he was further influenced by the ideals expressed in these writings when drafting the Declaration of Independence. The discussion before the original draft was said to have been expressed as "Life, Liberty and the Pursuit of Property" based on the wording from the First Continental Congress.

It was changed following the suggestion and debate brought forth by Benjamin Franklin of Pennsylvania to select the word 'Happiness' in place of 'Property'. Franklin believed the term 'property' reflected only those with land ownership, and not all the colonists owned land. He surmised that that 'property' was a "creature of society" and subject to taxation so as to finance civil society, and the Declaration should include the entirety of the colonials, regardless of an individual's possession and therefore the term 'Happiness' was chosen to better reflect the majority. The final version that we know today was adopted by the Second Continental Congress on July 4th, 1776.

In this ratified 'Declaration of Independence', the words 'the Pursuit of Happiness' were an inclusive vision of the concept of land and home ownership which was embraced by this broader expression of 'happiness', as well as embracing of the concepts of 'security of person', 'individual well-being' and 'personal freedom'. From this vision was born the idealism of the American Dream in the context of 'inalienable rights'.

As a testimony to this vision, the National Association of Realtors, founded in 1908 originally as the 'National Association of Real Estate Exchanges' has as the first lines in the Preamble to their Code of Ethics and Standards of Practice for the entire profession which reads:

"Under all is the land. Upon its wise utilization and widely allocated ownership depend the survival and growth of free institutions and of our civilization. Realtors® should recognize that the interests of the nation and its citizens require the highest and best use of the land and the widest distribution of land ownership. They require the creation of adequate housing, the building of functioning cities, the development of productive industries and farms, and the preservation of a healthful environment."

The American Dream of homeownership runs deep in the foundation of our nation. A perfect example is in one's childhood home. This place you grew up was a stable location that can be found in many citizens immediate recall when asked to go there in memory. Whether they lived in a house, apartment, condominium, or farm, wherever one grew up in America. It was a place, for better or for worse that you called home. I invite you as a reader at this point to pause, close your eyes, and get a picture of your childhood home.

Did you glimpse it for just a moment?

Homeownership embodies a fundamental value and measure of stability and serves as a springboard from which all other endeavors one engages in life is launched from: adults have a fundamental stability where they can rest their heads at night, and children have a place to grow. The goal of homeownership embodies personal freedom and stability, and is still a common goal for millions of Americans.

In the 1970's and early 1980's mortgage interest rates climbed in the U.S. to almost 18%. During that time in history, Land Contract home sales often exceeded conventional lending in many areas of the country, as seller-financing would often offer rates of 10-11%. Today, Land Contracts have taken on new role, serving as a bridge between a challenged financial history, and homeownership.

Despite the decline in real estate values across our nation in recent years, and the growing number of Americans with damaged credit, homeownership is still an obtainable goal by means of this 'bridge' of the Land Contract option.

This book, on the subject of financing your home by means of a Land Contract, Land Contracts will serve too many who read it as perhaps a source of hope as it may give you an understanding of the subject. From there, you will be able to determine if this is going to be the right course of action for you to pursue, or whether it is better to explore other alternatives that I suggest along the way in this book.

With property values at an all time low in many areas of the country, and current low interest rates there is no better time in history to pursue buying a home, and becoming a homeowner.

Certainly qualifying for a loan is more challenging these days, but these barriers can be overcome if one works with an experienced Realtor and other professionals in with the market in which you intend to buy. Low interest rates present an opportunity to a qualified buyer. In times of higher interest rates (which some experts say could be just around the corner) alternative approaches to financing property become popular. Seller-financing in the form of Land Contracts are one of these options that will gain rise in difficult times.

Let's return to the subject of the American Dream. As a Realtor, I have helped many people buy homes over the years. I have helped many, many people become homeowners even in a challenging market. In some cases, the option of the Land Contract (Otherwise best described as 'Seller Financing') was the right move for a particular buyer. In other cases we took a different route.

      This book is about exploring the possibilities of short term seller financing as an interim to arriving at conventional financing. We will discuss the outline of Land Contracts, and how they can be applied. We will also address details of the contract agreements, profiles of property that are ideal for such an agreement, remedies for default and even delve into the subject of credit repair. In this new addition, I have also added useful links and resources at the end. So, let's continue to examine the subject in the next chapter.

Chapter Two

What is a 'Land Contract'

or 'Contract for deed'?

തൎ

So what is a 'Land Contract' or 'Contract for Deed' and how does it work?

A "land contract", sometimes referred to as an "installment sale agreement" or "contract for deed", is a written contractual agreement between a seller and buyer of real estate in which the seller serves as the entity for financing, and the arrangement allows the buyer to acquire the property for an agreed-upon purchase price. The buyer follows an installment payment structure to pay off the loan.

Land contracts are common throughout the United States. In some states, they are referred to as 'Trust Deeds', 'Contract for Deed', 'Deeds of Trust', 'Notes', 'Private Money Mortgages' or 'Privately Held Mortgages'. Regardless of the name used, they all represent the same essential concept: a way of selling property where the buyer 'borrows' from or relies upon the seller for the financing rather than paying cash up front or obtaining a direct loan from a bank.

For the purpose of this book, as established earlier, the term 'Land Contract' will be used to designate 'Seller Financing'. Keep in mind that the terms vary in different regions, as well as the method, but the underlying concept is the same: 'Seller Financing'. It is a seller held note, not backed by a conventional banking or financial institution, but an individual or group under a land contract.

The seller throughout the contract all the way to the end holds the legal title to the property. The buyer is permitted to take possession of it for all defined purposes, but they do not gain final legal ownership until the loan is paid in full. The buyer has ownership rights, and is responsible for payment of taxes, insurance, and maintaining the property not unlike any written agreement with a mortgage company.

The buyer's ownership rights are subject to the conditions of a land contract being in effect, the payments not being in default and all payments being made. In some cases, an escrow account can be set up between the seller and buyer maintained by a third party to collect monthly contributions to these expenses, and disbursed annually or semi-annually when the bills come due.

The agreed upon purchase price of the sale is commonly paid over time in periodic installment payments. This frequently includes balloon payment at some future time period defined to make the time length of payments shorter than a customary commercial loan, which usually has no final balloon payment. Commonly the balloon payments are within a set time frame within the land contract agreement to be reached in two to five years, depending on the amount of the loan, but can be as much as ten years. This is a negotiable point between both parties, and can be set shorter or longer depending on the situation.

When the agreed upon purchase price has been paid inclusive of any interest, the seller is then required to transfer legal title of the property to the buyer. This is where it becomes important for a land contract to be recorded with the property registry of deeds in the area to maintain property rights for the buyer, and seller through the course of this transaction. This will be discussed further in a later chapter.

A down payment based on a percentage of the agreed upon sales price is usually required from the buyer to initiate a land contract, and this goes to the seller as the first major payment on the property to secure the buyers interests. The legal status of land contracts varies from state to state, and region to region. State laws should be reviewed in any situation where parties are considering such an agreement.

Chapter Three

An Outline of a Land Contract

ॐॐ

In 2010 I wrote a series of articles on the subject of Land Contracts in Michigan, which I published on a few of my blogs. Much of this material is included now in this book, along with new information, to present as complete a view of the subject as possible.

Most any Realtor in Michigan will attest it is quite common to be asked the question *"Do you have any homes for sale offering a Land Contract?"* I thought it might be helpful to provide some information to prospective buyers on the subject Land Contracts in Michigan, as well as in other states.

In the preceding sections we covered what a Land Contract was, a contractual agreement with a seller financed note. A Land Contract in simple terms is a form of financing from the seller of the property where the seller accepts a down payment, monthly payments and interest over a given period of time, and usually with a balloon payment at some point. A balloon payment is the entirety of the balance of the loan paid in one settlement at a predetermined point in the future.

A 'balloon' occurs after a specified period of time, where the final balance is either due in full, or the parties renegotiate the interest rate for another period. Land Contracts in Michigan, for example, are considered a legal transfer of ownership, and the buyer retains all property rights. The buyer can live in the house, make improvements and can even file for homestead property tax exemption. This may vary in other states, depending on how this is interpreted. One should consult the laws pertaining to the state the Land Contract is being executed in.

The seller in a Land Contract retains the title until the final payment is made, at which point the title is transferred to the buyer. There are some conditions that would limit the ability of a seller to offer a Land Contract as a term of the sale. One of these conditions is if the seller already has an existing mortgage on the home.

If there is an existing mortgage, then selling a home through land contract may not be possible, as many mortgages include a 'due on sale clause' in the mortgage. This language restricts the borrower from selling the home under such a system.

If the mortgagee were to engage in a Land Contract agreement with a buyer, and not disclose fact of a mortgage, the outcome could be less than desirable. The mortgagee could be forced to pay for the note in full to their lender for violating this agreement, and if unable to, forfeit the home if taken to court. The unknowing "buyer" of this Land Contract would of course lose all investment and ownership interests.

It is logical to assume that most sellers would not be willing to assume this risk. So the best condition for a seller, who wants to consider a land contract as a sales option, is if they own the house outright absent of liens, and are willing to accept a Land Contract proposal. However, it should be noted, not all mortgages prohibit reselling it on Land Contract, so in some cases it could be a viable option. However, it may be a risk for the buyer, should the seller default on the mortgage payments.

The original mortgage would have controlling interest on the ownership of the property should the mortgagee (seller) ever default. The Land Contract would only have the option of buying the first mortgage in full to assume ownership, or walk away and lose their investment. One should always owe less on the mortgage than the selling price of the Land Contract for this to be even considered an option.

On the other side of the transaction, many prospective buyers seeking Land Contracts in Michigan that I have quizzed about this are of the belief that they can just sign some papers and move in and start making payments. Many I have spoken to over the years are seeking an alternative to renting, and have misinformation that a Land Contract is as easy as signing a 'Rent to Own' agreement much like one may purchase furniture. This is the 'Urban Legend' of Land Contracts as described earlier. Many have no savings, or funds for a down payment, and sometimes no sustainable income that they can prove that would make them a good investment risk for the seller.

Often these buyers are in a poor financial condition, or perhaps recovering from one, and they are eager to accept any deal they can get, which makes them a potential target for fraud, which I will discuss in more detail later in this book. As a general rule, if you have no savings, no funds and no sustainable income, a Land Contract is not a good option unless you are working with a relative who will agree more flexible terms for you. However, this is a special circumstance.

Additionally many buyers do not realize that land contracts are often offered with higher interest rates, and a sales price of the home at fair market value, as the seller's goal is to make it a profitable venture if they are going to carry a personal mortgage with an individual, particularly with an individual they only have a business relationship with.

As a Realtor, I have taken many who were seeking a Land Contract initially to a reputable lender, and managed to help them repair their credit issues and get them approved for financing. A local loan officer in most cases can offer them better terms, with lower interest rates using current loan programs. However, sometimes a Land

Contract is the best way to go, if the credit repair will require a long period of time, say, two years. So if it works for the buyer and seller, it should be explored as a viable option.

When working on a Land contract, it is important for both parties in the transaction to know some key information so as to help them avoid future trouble with title and ownership. There are many points to the buying and selling process with Land Contracts that an experienced Realtor can help you with. One might also consult an attorney for legal review and advice.

Wisdom and experience would suggest that one should examine a few basic points when approaching such a transaction. In the next chapters, I outline component parts of a Land contract, as well as provide a list for both the buyer and seller sides of a transaction. When reading this you will see that each side has a unique perspective, in accordance with their specific interests in the transaction. To begin, let's examine the key components of a Land Contract, and what each means.

Chapter Four

Key Components of a Land Contract

ॐॐ

The essential key component of a land contract is people. Property is secondary really in the agreement, because without people, nothing happens in terms of the property changing hands. People make an agreement and devise a structured set of guidelines in which to follow setting up steps to follow so the property can change hands.

These guidelines become a form of regular practice through application, and get passed on into what is called *standard practice* or sometimes become law. Land Contracts were formed essentially in the same manner at their beginning.

The earliest forms of contracts were in the form of 'verbal agreements'. In fact, verbal contract still exist today. You maybe even made one today if you ate at a restaurant.

Now, you might be thinking "*Really? What contract did I make there? I just ate some food!*" However, even ordering food at a restaurant involves a contract of sorts.

Essentially whenever you order food at a restaurant, you enter into a verbal agreement that implies that they will serve you the food of your choice, and you agree to pay the bill for that food and service before you leave. That is a basic example of a verbal contract. A service is exchanged, or a product, or both, usually over a short period of time.

If someone were to engage in a verbal contract between friends on the purchase of land, for example, they could verbally agree on a price and then a monthly payment. However, if the verbal agreement goes on too long, one side might claim they *forgot* and decide not to fulfill the agreement, or change their mind, etc.

Also consider what can happen to a verbal contract if one of the people agreeing to the terms dies, or has an accident that leaves them incapable of fulfilling the agreement? There can be many circumstances or changes that can occur over time to make a verbal contract unstable for use over a long period of time.

So with that we can see that a written agreement become necessary the longer or larger a transaction becomes. The moment 'Time' is entered into an agreement, it become necessary to put things into a written form to compensate for the broad range of variables and unpredictable circumstances that can happen over time. Even with a written agreement, one must think in terms of the future in hopes to cover all possible variables.

Imagine for a moment the 'Wild West'. Two people wanted to transact business on a piece of land, and worked out a written agreement with payments they both agreed to initially. As problems came along, both learned from the experience, and either hired another person to help them (usually an attorney) to help them look at the arrangement to see how they could re-write it to define what should happen in certain circumstances.

What if one of the two dies before it is completed, one asks? What then? Let's assume they finished this initial agreement and then later wanted to transact business on a piece of land again, but this time there is a house on it. Consider this for a moment, as this introduces a lot of new variables.

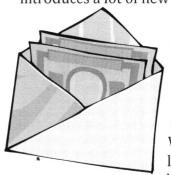

What happens if someone does not pay, can they be removed? What happens if they do not want to go? What happens if the place burns down, is stampeded with cattle or washed away in a flood? What if the married couple who live there get divorced, and one kicks the other out and the other refuses to pay for the home, and the one remaining in it cannot?

Can you imagine all of these kinds of scenarios? These kinds of thing become components in a contract because usually somewhere along the line they happened to someone. It became necessary to have these rules written into the agreement so that everyone understands the rules before going into the agreement.

Land Contract agreements can last years. Sometimes people make agreements, and forget what was agreed to. That is why agreements get written down, and that is why components in a contract define what should happen in the event something does happen. However, it does not just cover what might happen, it also factors in what everyone involved in agrees will happen too.

So let's look at some of the key components of a land contract from that perspective for a moment. There are several key components of a basic Land Contract. Every State in the U.S. will have variations on these, as well as additional components not listed here. The following chapter provided to give the reader a starting point of some of the common sections found in such this type of sellers financing agreement.

It should be noted that a Land Contract is not a 'Purchase Agreement'. A Purchase Agreement is a written agreement between a buyer and a seller outlining the terms of the sale. The Land Contract is the agreement in detail of the seller financing, and related terms. The Purchase Agreement will cover disclosures, sales price, time of execution, inspections, etc. It will also define the terms of the Land Contract as it relates to interest rate, length of time, balloon, etc. I will cover more on Purchase Agreements in a later chapter.

It is recommended that every transaction have a purchase agreement that all parties sign, in addition to the Land Contract itself, as this will further define the terms of the sale, time frames, etc. A local Realtor or attorney can help you with this.

Some of the key components of a Land Contract are defined in the following sections:

People Involved in the Contract

The "Parties" in the contract is usually the first item to define. This is the 'people' involved in the transaction, and includes the full legal names of the people (and their addresses) that are entering into the contract. It is recommended that the names match the exact legal identifications, such as a driver's license. This would include the middle initials and middle names where applicable. Avoid the use of nicknames in a legal document. A party can also be another entity such as a: Limited Liability Company, Corporation, Non-Profit, Partnership or some other legal group entity. In case like this, the contract will want to reference the documents that establish this legal entity, such as: corporate papers, articles of organization, etc.

The "Seller" is the person who is selling the property and is usually listed first. The "Purchaser" is the one purchasing (buying) the property and is usually listed in sequence after the Seller on the documents.

Legal Description

When a seller is agreeing to sell vacant land, residential or some other form of commercial property, the Seller is agreeing in the contract to convey (sell) to the Purchaser a very specifically described parcel of land. This description must be exact. When the purchase is completed and paid off, this should match the description on the deed. The city, village, or township of the property is noted, as well as county and state.

Using the mailing address of the property is not enough. The mailing address of a property is designed for use by the postal service, and is not the legal description.

There are several types of legal descriptions on property. Some define the location on the County parcels, including the city, township, village, etc. and down to the section of the grid and parcel number. Inner city properties will commonly have a shorter description defining a parcel and lot number.

Here is an example of what one of these looks like:

'Highland Hills Park E 1/2 Of Lot 51, All Of Lot 52'

Others describe it from a stake survey marking a point of beginning, and measuring out the boundaries of the defined land. These are common in rural properties.

Here is an example of one of these looks like:

'Athens Twp/T4s R8w, Sec. 22: Beg At Pt N24deg 25'e 641.24 Ft From A Pt 1631.7 Ft E Of W 1/4 Pst On E & W 1/4 Ln Of Sec., Th S24deg 25'w 96 Ft. N65deg 31'w 265 Ft M/L To Ctr Ln Of Hwy Ne'ly Alng Sd CtR Ln 95 Ft S65deg 35'e 265 Ft M/Lto P.O.B. (Sub To R.O.W. In The Nw'ly 100 Ft Thereof).'

This last one is called a 'Metes and Bounds' legal description. One does not need to become a surveyor to understand this subject, as long as they make sure that the legal description on the contract matches what is on the deed. You can see from this example that they can be comprehensive, so it is vital that it conforms exactly to the property being sold.

As the purchase includes not only the soil, vegetation, trees, water, etc. throughout the parameters defined in the legal description, the Seller also conveys such things as any buildings, easements, tenements, improvements and appurtenances.

- **Buildings**: Any structure on the land, including the house, garage, sheds, pole barns, etc.

- **Easements**: A right to cross over access or otherwise use someone else's land for a specified purpose. This can be shared driveway between two adjoining homes, for example.

- **Tenements**: Any room or rooms forming a separate residence within a block of apartments or house.

- **Improvements:** Any structures on the property or additions to the property that add value, such as trees or a swimming pool for example.

- **Appurtenances:** Pertaining to something that attaches. In real estate law this describes any restriction or right which goes with a property, such as an easement to gain access across the neighbor's parcel. Another example might be a covenant (agreement) against blocking the neighbor's view.

In short, the Seller conveys everything that is permanently affixed to the property, as well as all the above rights and restrictions as applicable. A good way to look at this is as anything screwed, bolted, glued or nailed down as remaining with the home as a 'fixture'. This will include any structures on the land as well.

Anything that can be detached with a simple plug or hook, wheeled off or un-hung from a nail are non-fixtures. This can include appliances, and will depend as to whether they are affixed or not based on the above description. For example: a dishwasher is often regarded as a fixture, as it is screwed or bolted in, whereas a refrigerator is not, as it is simply plugged in.

Price and Terms of Payment

This area should contain all the numerical values concerning sales price, costs and also timeframes in terms of dates:

The date of the Contract is here at the beginning as well. Interest starts to "accrue" (begins being owed to the Seller) starting from the date typed in, at the top of the contract. Consequently, when the first payment is due, one month's interest is usually already owed, since it is customarily paid in arrears (paying at the end of a period of which it is incurred).

The 'numerical values' will include such things as the final purchase price and the dollar value of down payment. It will also include the beginning balance in the contract (this in calculated as the purchase price minus the dollar value of the down payment). It will also establish the monthly payment (or in some cases the annual or semi-annual payment), what the agreed upon interest rate is (this is commonly defined in terms of an annual rate).

The contract will further defined when the date of the 'balloon' payment (if any) shall fall, and specific date that the first payment shall be due, along with which day of the month future payments will be due throughout the contract. A 'balloon payment' is defined further below, but is essentially a point defined in the future where the entire note becomes due.

Purchase Price - The 'agreed upon Purchase price' (sometimes defined legally as "consideration") is negotiated between the Seller and the Purchaser. Properties sold on a land contract commonly are sold for more in terms of sale value in the agreed upon purchase price than properties that are sold for cash simply because the Seller is providing the financing, which is what is considered all-important to the buyer. If the seller has another note the purchase price should be higher than the balance owed.

Down Payment - The down payment is customarily 10% to 20% of the agreed upon purchase price. It represents funds that the seller does not have to collect in the process of the purchase, and it also represents the Purchaser's commitment to buying the property. Sometimes, non-cash down payments (barter items such as used cars, boats, tractors, snowmobiles, applied rent, other property, etc.) can be used as a form of a down payment (full or in part) when no other options

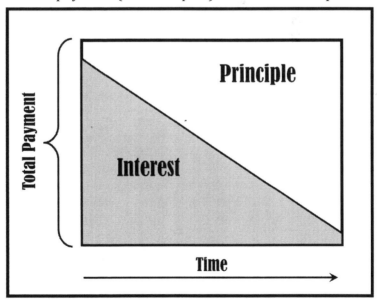

are available. There can be very creative ways to structure a sale. These options are not readily available through a conventional lending institution. This is a distinct advantage of a Land Contract.

Balance Remaining - This defines the amount that is the purchase price subtracting the numerical value of the down payment. The balance remaining will decrease each month with every payment made by the new home owner. An 'amortization schedule' shows how the balance will be reduced if monthly payments are made on time. An 'amortization schedule' is best defined as: "complete schedules of loan payments, showing the amount of principal and the amount of interest that comprise each payment". Often the agreement references the amortization schedule which is usually a printed attachment to the finalized Land Contract.

Monthly Payment - The monthly payment formula is most commonly approximately 1% to 1.5% of the beginning or starting balance defined on the contract. If after the down payment the Seller is owed $50,000 by the Purchaser, the monthly payment will probably be in the neighborhood of $500 to $750.

The smaller in size of the monthly payment, the longer in time it will take to settle the final value or remaining balance owed in land contract and the larger the monthly payment the faster the remaining balance can be paid off.

Payment Due Date - It is the date defined for the initial payment being due and also refers to the specific day of the month each consecutive payment agreed to be due. This date is a negotiable point between buyer and seller. Failing to make payment on a due date could also result in late fees, and these will also be defined in the agreement.

Grace Period - In some contracts, a grace period is defined. This allows the Purchaser a few days each month during which payments are due and not be considered in default. Some contracts will establish a late fee in the agreement if the payment is not received by the defined time or within the timeframe established as the 'grace period'. Grace periods and/or late fee clauses are customarily included at the end of the contract as miscellaneous provisions, but are none the less important to note.

Home buyers can commonly mistake the last day of the grace period as the payment due date. One needs to be cognizant that even though a late fee is not being charged, the payment is still in terms of contract performance *late*. Although a Land Contract holder is not likely to report to a credit agency, they might. Also, if you ever need a good reference on your performance, pay on time, and always before the grace period.

Balloon Payment - A *balloon payment* is the term used for a lump sum, final payment on the contract. Balloon clauses usually call for the final payment to be made on a specified date. A contract may contain a clause that reads something like, "the entire purchase price plus defined interest shall be paid in full within three years from the date hereof, anything herein to the contrary notwithstanding". This is what is referred to as a 'balloon' in the contract (a three year balloon, in this example).

If the Purchaser fails to make a balloon payment when required, this most often will constitute a default on the contract, unless some other provision is provided. It is common to see a balloon payment defined as either: 2, 3, 5 or even 10 years depending on what is negotiated. A balloon payment can define that the remaining balance be simply paid minus interest, or plus interest, so this is important to note.

Defined Interest Rate - The *interest rate* is a percentage rate commonly defined as an annual term, (e.g., 9%, 11%, etc). When one records each payment made, interest is then calculated for the payment period (usually monthly) by multiplying the interest rate by the remaining balance due. It is then calculated each consecutive payment as the annual interest amount by the number of payments to be made each year.

Here is an example as reflected on an amortization schedule with an 11% interest rate on a loan of $100,000 over a 15 year period, with the first 12 payments represented here:

Month	Payment	Interest	Principle	Balance
1	$1,136.00	$916.67	$219.93	$99,780.07
2	$1,136.00	$914.67	$221.95	$99,558.12
3	$1,136.00	$912.62	$223.98	$99,334.14
4	$1,136.00	$910.56	$226.04	$99,108.10
5	$1,136.00	$908.49	$228.11	$98,879.99
6	$1,136.00	$906.40	$230.20	$98,649.79
7	$1,136.00	$904.29	$232.31	$98,417.48
8	$1,136.00	$902.16	$234.44	$98,183.04
9	$1,136.00	$900.01	$236.59	$97,946.45
10	$1,136.00	$897.84	$238.76	$97,707.69
11	$1,136.00	$895.65	$240.95	$97,466.74
12	$1,136.00	$893.45	$243.15	$97,223.59

This calculated value which it the total interest for the period, is subsequently deducted from the payment as shown in the example above. The rest of the payment is known as the 'principal' portion of the payment and is then subtracted from the adjusted remaining principal balance as the balance is reduced following the terms of the contract.

As an additional note on this, it is common for uninformed buyers to take issue with a higher interest rate that a seller is offering, which exceeds perhaps a local loan rate. There really is no exact correlation between interest rates on a loan offered by a bank or credit union and interest rates on a Land Contract.

Land Contracts are typically higher, as you are working with a private seller. It should be understood, however, that the seller, lacking the resources of a large lender, assumes more of a risk in offering financing. Typically this risk is compensated with a higher interest rate, a larger down payment or both.

Taxes and Insurance

The party who becomes responsible for paying the tax and insurance payments on the property depends upon what is defined in the terms of the land contract. Property taxes can be in the form of a singular payment, or divided into separate bills for State, County, Township or Village, depending on the practices followed in your area.

Check with your local Assessor's office for details on this. Insurance typically is just a homeowner's coverage, however in certain areas of the country flood insurance or 'Wind' insurance may be an additional requirement.

The three common methods to structure the taxes and insurance payments on the property, and define who is responsible for this and what method will be used is as follows:

1) The Purchaser pays the required taxes and insurance; or

2) The Seller pays the required taxes and insurance and then adds the exact value of amounts paid back to the balance on the contract; or

3) The Purchaser makes monthly payments to an escrow account held by the Seller and the Seller pays the required taxes and insurance premiums out of this account.

Method 1: Purchaser pays the Taxes and Insurance premiums

Customarily the most common of these methods is that the Purchaser is the party responsible for paying the taxes and insurance premiums on the property. A typical clause in a land contract where the Purchaser pays the property taxes and insurance premiums is often written as this:

"The Purchaser agrees to pay all assessments and taxes hereafter levied on said premises ..."

Method 2: Seller pays and re-adds the amount spent back to contract principle balance.

Since failure to pay either the tax or the insurance bills can seriously place at risk the value of the property and investment defined in the land contract (imagine trying to collect payments on an uninsured home that was destroyed in a flood, destroyed in a storm or was lost in a fire!).

For this reason, some Sellers demand to pay the property tax and insurance premiums themselves. Following making payments on these bills, the Sellers just add the expenses of insurance and taxes back onto the end balance of the land contract at the time that the tax payments and insurance premiums are paid, and then send a statement to the buyer.

These statements can be monthly, quarterly or annually as defined in the agreement. Contracts of this type are sometimes referred to as 'Back Loaded' or in some cases referred to as amounts 'Added Back'. This may be a viable option if a seller lives out of State, and wants reassurance that these are paid. It can also be a good option for someone who lacks the time, ability or resources to verify the payments are made, as when one is selling the home for an elder parent in a nursing home, for example.

When using this option, the monthly payment will commonly be increased with an estimated amount to cover the approximated one-twelfth of the estimated taxes along with the required premiums for insurance. These payments are treated just as if the entire amount of each payment was for principal and interest, with the added larger value to cover the estimated one-twelfth fee for the property taxes and insurance.

This can make the balance on the contract drop at a more rapid rate that it customarily would. However, one must also factor in that when the tax and insurance bills are delivered to the Seller, the Seller remits payment to them and then adds the value of the funds spent to the end balance due on the land contract.

Therefore, the final remaining balance on the land contract, after having been reduced each month more than it normally would be due to the larger payments, is then re-adjusted upward when the amounts for property taxes and insurance premiums are added back to the contract balance.

Method 3: Seller Pays Taxes and Insurance out of Amounts Put in Escrow

A third method to address how the property taxes and insurance premiums are paid is similar to Method 2. In this method the Purchaser pay approximately one-twelfth of the estimated property taxes and insurance premiums in addition to each monthly payment installment. The Seller places these added funds into a special account each month, in what is called an "escrow account" to remit payment for these bills as they are due.

If the escrow account ever becomes insufficient to pay these bills, the Seller notifies the Purchaser and a new adjusted higher value of the escrow payment is then required to be included along with the next monthly payment. Compliance for this is defined in the contract.

Commonly adjustments are made annually when using this method.

Sometimes escrow accounts can be maintained by using a separate entity. Some banks or Title companies might offer this service in your area. In any event, there are precise accounting procedures that must be followed with escrow accounts, and it is recommended that you consult with a Certified Public Accountant regarding the laws pertaining to your State.

Seller's Right to Mortgage

The Seller has the right to borrow against his or her remaining equity in the property sold. In other words, if the Seller owned a $50,000 property free and clear and then sold it to the Purchaser with a $10,000 down payment, the Seller initially has the right to collect $40,000 (his or her remaining equity in the property) and he or she may borrow money by allowing a lender to put a senior lien on the property (ahead of the Purchaser's interest in the property) for up to $40,000.

However, since the Seller must be in a position at all times to convey the Deed to the property when the Purchaser makes the final payment on the contract, the Seller can never owe more on the property than he or she is owed by the Purchaser.

To protect the Purchaser from any debts that the Seller may have against the property, the Seller must provide notice of any such mortgage and its terms in a certified letter to the Purchaser.

The Purchaser also has the right to make the payments for the Seller on any debt for which the Seller is in default. Any such payment made by the Purchaser, of course, will be deducted from the monthly payment owed by the Purchaser to the Seller.

As an example: If a home one is buying receives a foreclosure notice from the original lender, one has a right to pay that payment directly to prevent default of one chooses.

Once again to summarize, the Seller must never owe on the property more than he or she is owed. To engage in such an agreement otherwise is to make for an inequitable transaction, and invite future complications which could have legal ramifications.

Purchaser's Duties to Maintain Premises

It is the Purchaser's duty to protect and maintain the value of the property he or she is buying until the final balance on the land contract is settled in full. Therefore a clause defining this duty is included in most contracts, and it is important because it is the value of the property that keeps the Purchaser making payments.

Should the Purchaser ever go into default and be required to return the home to the seller by means of forfeiture or foreclosure, it is this retained value of the condition of the property that enables a Seller to re-sell it without a loss.

Most land contracts require the Purchaser to notify the Seller in writing before the Purchaser or any third party alters or demolishes any buildings, commits waste (neglects or damages the property or allows it to be used in a way that would lessen resale value) or removes and/or makes improvements on the premises in a way which may lesson, alter or ultimately diminish the property's value in terms of resale.

One cannot dispose of hazardous waste on the property either, such as disposing of oil, fuel, industrial waste, radioactive material, etc. Disposing of such chemicals can affect ground water, and well systems, and can greatly reduce the value of a property to say the least. Abandonment of old vehicles and violations of city ordinances concerning property condition could also fall into this category, for example.

Seller's Duty to Provide Proof of Title and Convey (or 'Deed over') Premises

Once the buyer has made the final payment on the land contract without default, the Seller is required to convey the property by signing over a Deed to the exact property defined in the legal description as the property.

Upon delivering the Deed, the Seller often additionally delivers an 'abstract of title' (A shortened or condensed history, taken from public records or documents, of the ownership of a piece of land, most often prepared by an attorney) or a policy of title insurance demonstrating that the property is free and clear from any liens that the Seller may have remaining or had in prior history on the property.

The party that is required to cover the expense of the insurance should be agreed upon when the terms of the land contract is initiated.

It is recommended for the protection of both parties that they obtain title insurance on the property being sold, before they finalize a Land Contract agreement.

This is particularly important for the buyer to verify the seller is indeed the rightful owner of the property. More on this will be covered in a later chapter concerning prevention of fraud.

It is the Purchaser's responsibility to record the Deed. The fee is nominal and recording the Deed will show as a matter of public record that the Purchaser is the new owner of the property.

Assignment of the Contract

A Seller commonly wants to retain the right to freely assign his or her interest in the land contract to another party. This means that a seller can sell the Land Contract to another investor if they choose. (An exception might be if the Seller is still making payments on the property themselves and the original contract governing that purchase restricts or prevents the Seller's from being able to assign.)

The Purchaser in a land contract often has the right to assign his or her interest in the contract; however it is most commonly restricted to 'only after obtaining written permission from the Seller'. Essentially, one cannot have someone else take over the responsibility of the Land Contract payments and absolve oneself from any liability in the event of future default.

This clause is a protection for the Seller. It exists simply due to the fact that a Seller may only have sold the property to the buyer on the strength of the Purchaser's credit rating, employment stability, or character, along with other factors.

When this Purchaser then proposes a change to a new party, who will then become the primarily responsible person for performing on payments to the Seller in a land contract, the Seller is entitled to and given the right to review, make examination and evaluate this new purchaser and approve such a change to the original agreement in writing.

Further, any approved assignment by the Purchaser to this new purchaser quite often does not release the original Purchaser from the obligation to perform under the contract should the new purchaser default on the original land contract.

Default

If the Purchaser fails to make payment or perform any significant part of the contract it is then considered to be in 'default'. The Seller quite often has the right, after notifying the Purchaser in writing of the exact nature of the default, to regard all previous payments made to the date of the default on the contract as simply 'rental payments' made by the Purchaser. State laws vary on this point from State to State. Some jurisdictions have specific guidelines regarding default on land contracts, so be sure to check with legal professionals.

If the default continues, the Seller has the right to declare the remaining balance due and payable, and if the default is not then cleared up or the contract is not paid in full, the Seller can begin steps to regain possession of the property. Improvements made to the property by the Purchaser then become the Seller's property.

Most often default by the Purchaser is commonly understood to be failure to make timely payments.

However, default can also include failure to pay insurance premiums and therefore adequately insure the property, failure to pay property taxes as they become due or failure to properly safeguard against damage and waste or maintain the value property. See later chapter on remedies for default.

Miscellaneous Provisions

Most all contracts close with a list or section of defined 'miscellaneous provisions' regarding where the notices and payments should be mailed, which state law is governing the specific agreement, and so forth. The common provisions in a basic or standard pre-printed land contract are secondary to importance of typed provisions at the end of a negotiated contract, as these represent the unique terms negotiated between buyer and seller. Be certain to read, interpret and enforce these typed provisions carefully.

Signatures and Notarization

In order for a Land Contract to be recorded in the local county records in the area that the property is located, you are required to have the contract notarized by a licensed notary. This does not necessarily require a notary from that State, but their license must be enforce and current. There is usually no fee for this service, and if there is one fee, it is usually nominal. Some states prohibit a notary from charging a fee.

Witnesses will often be needed as signature in the contract, and they will need to be available to observe the signing of the contract when it happens. This is also done in front of a notary.

It is further recommended that identification of all parties, including the witnesses be obtained for the records. This is particularly important for the seller. This verification of identification for the records can be a copy of their driver's license or passport, for example. Most attorney offices and title companies require this now as part of the Homeland Security Regulations.

Chapter Five

What a Land Contract is *Not*

৵৽৹

When discussing the subject of land contracts and how they work, it would also be prudent to discuss what a Land Contract is not.

A land contract is not the same as renting. In renting a home, one is buying time to remain in the residence. It is limited to the time frame defined in the terms of the lease. As a renter, you are using your time to reside there or make use of the property while making payments to do so. When your contract with the landlord is up, you can move or sign a new one and continue. However, when it is over you have no ownership interest in the home or property.

With a land contract, you are buying a home with monthly installment payments plus interest. When the terms of the contract are complete in most cases you:

- Pay off the remaining note by refinancing.

- Pay the balance off in cash, or

- Renegotiate a new land contract with the seller on the remaining balance (if the seller is willing).

If you do not, then depending on the terms of the land contract, you could be in default and lose all ownership interest in the home. This means that any investment to that point could be lost due to default on the contract. (See later chapter on Default)

Ultimately, when all agreements are finally met, you own the home. The key phrase in this last statement is "when all agreements are finally met". Failing to perform on payments, failing to pay the insurance, or property taxes, failing to maintain the home per the agreement can be considered in default of the agreement and you may lose all of your investment.

A renter who moves often and tires of a location after a short time is not likely to be the correct candidate for a land contract. Buying a home on a land contract requires commitment.

When renting a home, if one encounters problems with the plumbing, heating, etc. one calls the landlord who will arrange for repair. The property owner in accordance with most lease agreements is therefore the responsible party to resolve the repair.

In a land contract, you are the owner. You alone are responsible for the repairs. Monthly income and budget should factor in these costs, and planning in the event they do happen. When renting, one does not have to factor in this planning. The planning is done by the owner (landlord) and you simply pay your rent and go about your daily life.

With home ownership, one has to factor in the planning for the upkeep of the home. There are various categories of maintenance in the average home:

- Weekly/Monthly maintenance: Cleaning, trash removal, etc.

- Quarterly/Semi-Annual maintenance: Changing of furnace filters or smoke detector batteries for example.

- Seasonal maintenance: Closing storm windows in the fall, raking leaves, draining swimming pools, sprinkler systems in the fall, and turning the on again in the spring. Mowing the lawn in the summer and shoveling snow in the winter, for example.

- 1-3 Year maintenance actions: cleaning a well, pumping a septic tank, etc.

There can be a variety of maintenance in a home. Every climate or location will require different actions. It is important to understand and learn what those are for the area you are moving to if you are unfamiliar. It is always a good idea to consult with people who live in the area.

Homeowners Insurance can protect you against major damage from disasters (Hurricanes, storm damage, fire, etc.). However, there are still deductibles required by insurance companies. It is important to know what these are.

A higher deductible on insurance can mean a lower monthly payment, but more out-of-pocket expense for the homeowner in the event of a major repair. A lower deductible will mean a higher monthly payment, but a lower out of pocket expense if faced with a major repair. Insurance rates are also impacted by the credit worthiness of the buyer, and insurance providers check credit bureaus for this information.

There is also a product called a Home Warranty that one can buy as a homeowner that can offset the cost of major repairs. Usually home warranties have an annual fee to keep them current. Additionally, utility companies sometimes offer service plans for interior repairs on gas lines and appliances, and add a fee to your monthly bill. These, too, can be helpful in protecting one from unexpected costs when confronted with needful repairs.

Despite all these safeguards, there may be home repairs and expenses that one must prepare for when it comes to monthly budgeting.

When one rents a home, the landlord as property owner is responsible for payment of taxes and insurance. Under a land contract arrangement, you are the homeowner, and in most cases you are responsible for the annual taxes and homeowners insurance, which is usually above and beyond the agreed upon monthly payment with the seller.

Most land contracts either require proof of this being paid annually to the seller, or have a prearranged escrow account established in which a portion of your monthly payment is placed. Annual premiums and tax bills are paid from it. Although not common, one can also structure the contract so the seller pays the taxes, and insurance, and this is added onto the back end of the principle. I will go into more detail about this later when discussing components of a land contract.

'Rent-to-own' is a concept that has its origin in the furniture business, and the term has been used to loosely describe what is traditionally called a 'lease with an option to buy' arrangement in real estate, also known as a 'lease option'.

A 'lease option' is essentially a rental agreement combined with a sales agreement for a home. A buyer who is not in a position to purchase right now for whatever reason can often use this as an option.

For example, a prospective buyer moving into a new area might not be certain he or she will be staying in the location, or be transferred with their company in a few years. When real estate values are rising, this can be a tool used to secure a price today with essentially a post dated closing date in the future, and the buyer secures this agreement for the seller with an 'option fee'. They then arrange a rental agreement, and they move in and rent the home.

The option agreement is usually arranged so that the buyer has the option of executing the purchase agreement in the future, and the fee is applied to the purchase of the home. If they choose to decline on this, usual arrangements are that the option fee in its entirety or in part goes to the seller if the buyer chooses to not execute the option.

The seller receives the option fee in exchange for the taking the home off the market for the lease period, and the buyer pays this fee for the right to buy the home at the market price of today. Lease option agreements include that the money paid for rent or a portion of it goes towards an accumulated value towards the down payment for that future sale.

A land contract differs from a lease option in that there is no lease involved. With a lease option, during the lease period, the buyer is regarded as a tenant. They do not pay taxes or homeowners insurance, and they also do not have a recorded interest in the deed. With a land contract, the buyer pays the taxes, insurance and has a recorded ownership interest in the deed as it is, in fact, a private note.

For the duration of a lease option, the seller of the property is a landlord, and the buyer is a tenant. This will make both parties subject to all the State laws of this arrangement, despite the option and post dated sales agreement.

For example, if the location you live requires annual inspections on rental units, the property would be subject to those regulations. If a buyer paying rent on a lease option defaults on the agreement, they can be evicted in accordance with tenant/landlord laws of that State, as the buyer is not the homeowner.

In the event of a default of the terms of a Land Contract, removing a person from the property follows an entirely different procedure and varies from State to State. It is commonly referred to as a 'Recovery of Possession after Land Contract Forfeiture'. The speed in which this is done will vary depending on what State you reside in, and what redemption regulations exist within that State.

Some States permit a period of time (For example in Illinois it is 90 days, in New Jersey it is 10 days, and in States like Delaware, Florida and Ohio there are zero days as of this writing) called a "redemption period" where an individual in default can pay off the note in its entirety before having to surrender the property.

To determine whether a land contract or contract for deed applies to the State laws concerning redemption periods, it is recommended that you consult an attorney or review the redemption laws of the State in question.

Here is a website you can refer to check the foreclosure procedures and redemption laws by state: *www.realtytrac.com/foreclosure-laws/foreclosure-laws-comparison*

The best summary definition available on a description of a Land contract is as follows:

An agreement between a buyer and seller of a property (residential, commercial or agricultural) in which the buyer makes payments toward full ownership (as with a mortgage), however in a land contract, the title or deed is held by the owner until the full payment is made at some future date, usually ending with a balloon payment.

Perhaps the most important thing to understand about what a Land Contract is not, is that it is not a free ride to 'avoid the system' of having to get your financial house in order.

It is important to realize that although a person with poor credit can get into a land contract agreement, there is a responsibility on their part to improve their credit within a time frame. A majority of land contract arrangements have a balloon payment at some point, and unless one has a resource for cash to settle the balance, one is going to need to prepare to be able to qualify for a loan.

Chapter Six

Land Contract Basic Tips for Success

൚ൟ

Selling or buying on a land contract can be an excellent way to sell or obtain a property quickly and at a good price. Conventional financing in the last 5 to 7 years has become even more costly, more difficult to obtain and often time consuming. Seller-financing will likely become even more popular if interest rates and lending restrictions remain tight.

It is estimated on a national scale that approximately 25% of property sold is now sold with some form of Seller financing, including both commercial and residential real estate.

If interest rates climb, the market will likely see more non-conventional financing methods used to convey property, and the Land Contract will be a good option for the seller.

When considering selling a property on land contract, here are some things that should be known. The way a contract is planned and written can have a bearing on its value in the future.

The Purchase Price

The purchase price is negotiated between the Seller and the Purchaser, but there are some property evaluation standards that can be used as the guideline for this negotiation process.

A basic initial method is to have two or three different real estate agents do a 'Comparative Market Analysis' (CMA) on the property, complete with three comparable sales, and three comparable active listing each.

Often called 'comparables', these are properties that are comparable to the subject property and can be used to acquire a range for its value on the market in the local marketplace.

The sold comparisons will help gauge the sales rate in the area, and the active listing comparisons will help gauge the current competition on the open market for similar properties. It is always best to factor in the 'Days on the Market' (DOM) for each of the active listing and sold comparisons, and these should be less than 90 days.

Too high a DOM will demonstrate the comparison is overpriced for the current market for example, and may not be a good representation to grant consideration to.

An average of these three analyses will usually give the Seller a fair indication of what the property is likely to sell for in the local market. This service is often free since the real estate agents will be competing for the opportunity to represent the seller in selling the property.

The agent you feel most comfortable with is the one you should list your property with.

Attempt to find the two or three agents that represent most of the listings in the area that your property is located. I would suggest that you avoid agents that specialize primarily in foreclosed properties, as their CMA will often reflect more of a foreclosure value than a fair market value.

A Realtor can tell you what the 'Fair Market Value' is in your area for the home, which can differ from the 'Appraisal Value'.

A Realtor can also check recent sales comparing homes similar to the one under consideration. Comparisons of size, number of bedrooms, location and similar amenities can all be evaluated to determine the Fair Market Value for home, as an example.

A good outline for comparison should be to select properties of similar size (general living area), number of bedrooms, number of baths, acreage or lot size, location (including school district), design, condition and sometimes age.

The range should be within a ½ to 1 mile radius in urban areas, 2-5 miles in suburban areas and within 10 miles preferably with rural locations. Comparable properties selected in this manner help narrow down ones similar to the one under consideration, often referred to as the 'subject' property in any report.

Another common approach, although does involve more upfront cost, is to hire an independent property appraiser to do a detailed appraisal on the property. This would include (as indicated above) at least three recently sold comparable properties within the last 3 to 6 months.

This method requires payment of their fees (often in a range of $200 to $350) but can provide a more authoritative review of value and is usually considered a better gauge of the true property value. The party paying this fee will need to be defined in the Purchase Agreement.

The Down Payment

A down payment is commonly a minimum of 10% to 20% of the agreed upon sales price defined in the Land Contract. This does not mean that a larger down payment cannot be paid, and if so this essentially means the Purchaser has more equity and has a smaller remaining balance, both of which can make the contract more secure.

A basic rule to consider is that with a larger down payment, the more the overall value a land contract is. The contracts length of time that it has been in existence also will affect the resale value of that contract, should the seller at a later date decide to sell the Land Contract to another investor.

As another note, Investors that acquire pre-established land contracts often prefer ones that have been in existence (seasoned) contracts. It is an indication that the Purchaser of the Land Contract making payments is a safe risk.

The best rule of thumb is: 'the higher the purchase price, the lower the percentage of down payment that could be considered. The lower the purchase price, the higher the down payment'. For example, a house that is selling for $500,000 may have a 10% down payment ($50,000) that is acceptable to the seller, whereas a house selling for $25,000 might want $5000 (20%). It all depends on what the seller feels comfortable with in the transaction.

The Interest Rate

Interest rates on a land contracts are at a minimum the equivalent to interest rates currently charged on mortgages by banks and credit unions for a moderate to high risk borrower based on credit report scores; preferably 1% - 2% higher, however it is not uncommon to see rates as much as 5% higher. This can be a negotiable point between parties.

There are legal interest rate maximums in most states for interest rates land contracts between individuals. Check with a legal professional or check with your State for details.

The Monthly Payment

A formula of 1% per month on the remaining balance at the time of purchase after one has deducted the down payment is a common formula. Let's look at this example:

$50,000 agreed upon sales price of the property

-$10,000 (20%) down payment

$40,000 balance due plus interest

$400 monthly payment (1% of remaining balance due); factor in the 1/12th amount of the estimated property taxes and insurance premiums.

When it comes to lower value land contracts amounts (for example below $25,000), a monthly payment greater than 1% of the remaining amount due is commonly selected.

To calculate the length of a land contract and what the monthly payment amounts should be, there are many free amortization calculators one can find online or even as apps for your phone.

This will allow you to punch in numbers, and make adjustments based on time, interest rate, and payment amount until you find something that works for both parties. One can also consult a title company for help with this. These tools or services are usually free.

Here is an example of the first 12 payments required on a monthly payment amortization scale over 15 years at an interest rate of 10%, on a purchase price of $50,000:

Month	Payment	Interest	Principle	Balance
1	$537.30	$416.67	$120.63	$49,879.37
2	$537.30	$415.66	$121.64	$49,757.73
3	$537.30	$414.65	$122.65	$49,635.08
4	$537.30	$413.63	$123.67	$49,511.41
5	$537.30	$412.60	$124.70	$49,386.71
6	$537.30	$411.56	$125.74	$49,260.97
7	$537.30	$410.51	$126.79	$49,134.18
8	$537.30	$409.45	$127.85	$49,006.33
9	$537.30	$408.39	$128.91	$48,877.42
10	$537.30	$407.31	$129.99	$48,747.43
11	$537.30	$406.23	$131.07	$48,616.36
12	$537.30	$405.14	$132.16	$48,484.20

As you can see, the balance progressively goes down with each payment, but by only the principle amount, not the interest.

Taxes and Insurance

Lending institutions generally divide a buyer's payment into 12 monthly payments. Thus, they will require the borrower to pay one-twelfth of the estimated yearly real estate taxes per month and the estimated insurance premiums in addition to the monthly payment.

At the close of a year, sufficient funds have accumulated in this special account from the twelve payments to pay the property taxes and annual insurance premium.

This is perhaps the most practical solution for the taxes and insurance payments on a land contract, but it does require a special escrow account be established.

Due to the fact that the land contracts span a period of time into the future, there will be variations in property taxes that will ascend and descend, so be certain to include a clause in the land contract that factors in increasing the payment to account for these variances.

Keep in mind that insurance rates are connected with a buyers credit score, so it is best to check with different insurance providers and compare rates. Additionally, some properties may require additional flood insurance or 'wind' insurance, etc.

A property may also have homeowner's association dues or fees, and sometimes parties will agree to have these escrowed as well.

Underlying Debt

If a Seller has a remaining balance of a mortgage on the property under consideration for a Land Contract, they do not necessarily have to pay off this mortgage. This can also be referred to as 'underlying debt'.

This *underlying debt* can also be in the form of a land contract to another party. Instead of paying off the underlying debt, they can in most cases continue to make monthly payments as agreed to in their mortgage.

This original obligation, however, is considered to be settled in full before the new seller can over own the property free and clear. Sellers should verify that the land contract or mortgage they are still making payments to and verify there is not a so-called "Due on Sale" clause requiring them to pay off the debt before they resell the property.

A good rule of thumb if working a sale that involves underlying debt is to have a Seller structure the land contract payment being received to be at least 25% greater than the payment they will continue to make on the original mortgage or note. The buyer may also want a clause in the Land Contract that requires the seller to demonstrate monthly, quarterly or annually that the underlying debt is being paid.

Amortization

The length of a land contract timeline is the contract's amortization schedule. The Land Contract's amortization takes into account the overall amount of the sale and the length of time to pay on the contract. It also factors in the monthly payment amount, as well as the interest rate being charged.

Therefore one can conclude that the higher the rate of interest and/or the smaller in size of the monthly payment, the longer the length of time for amortization will be. This is what brought into existence with many Land Contracts the use of a balloon payment, which essentially requires the contract be paid in full at a defined date, regardless of timeline.

Contracts with a 10 to 20 year span for amortization are frequently preferred to contracts with the longer 30 year span for amortization. Balloon payments are frequently established to be enforced at 2, 3, 5 or 10 years from the date the contract begins.

A final balloon payment can easily be calculated with an amortization calculator found for free in many places on the internet as defined earlier in this chapter. Deduct the total sum of principle payments made to date from the agreed upon purchase price of the Land Contract to obtain the balance of the balloon payment.

The Purchaser's Credit-worthiness

In conventional lending, a buyer is required to prove their credit worthiness. In Land Contract arrangements, a Seller has the same right to request the information from the Purchaser to demonstrate that they have an adequate source of income to perform on the land contract obligation.

The seller can also request references, verify employment and his or her annual income, and obtain a credit report showing a history of credit worthiness and how one is paying their current debts. If seller doing a review determines that the applicant has less than a commendable credit record, they very often will deny the right to sell or can increase the required amount of down payment and monthly payment in the amortization.

As a matter of standard administrative record-keeping, one should always keep on file a financial application filled out by the buyer, complete with social security number, date of birth and a copy of the purchasers legal ID, such as a driver's license or passport. This documentation on file is vital for the seller should a default occur, and legal action becomes necessary to pursue the buyer in a District Court System. One cannot file for a judgment or collect garnishment in many court systems without this data.

Memorandum of Land Contract

A Purchaser or Seller may not want to place in a recorded public record all of the financial details of a Land Contract transaction. The solution is to have a Memorandum of Land Contract be drafted, then signed by all parties, witnessed and notarized.

It is simply a single page that summarizes the terms of the sale, parties involved, sales price and date of the transaction along with the legal description of the property. It serves as a notification to all who review these County records that a Land Contract exists on the property.

In the recording this Memorandum in public records, both parties have notified interested public doing a record search that an agreement does exist regarding the sale of that property.

A Memorandum filing is additionally more cost effective than recording a multi-page land contract since Memorandums are typically only one page long. The purpose is that it serves as a legal notice of the existence of a Land Contract for anyone searching public records, but keeps the comprehensive details of the terms private for both parties.

Chapter Seven

Get it in Writing

࿊

The Purchase Agreement

A Purchase Agreement (PA) is a written agreement between parties to purchase a property. It defines the terms of the sale in many aspects, and defines which party is responsible for each aspect. It not only defines the property, and who the buyer and seller are, but it also stipulates conditions and when they are to be met. It will cover many of the points on the following list:

- The parties in the sale (Including realty offices representing either party, if any).

- Property description (Address, County and legal description).

- Sales Price

- Good faith deposit

- Types and terms of financing (In this case a Land Contract).

- Inspections (Including Well & Septic, electrical, plumbing, structural, pest and any other inspections deemed necessary by the buyer.)

- Property Survey (A process to determine the boundaries, dimensions and lines of a property.)

- Water access, rights, etc. associated with the property.

Possession

Home Warrantees (These are typically 12-18 month protection plans that will offset the cost of unexpected or unknown repairs, such as the failure of a furnace, air conditioning system, etc.)

Tax pro-rations (Defines who will pay for what portion of the current taxes due on the property. Most agreements have the seller pay up to the date of sale, and the buyer responsible for it from that point forward, but it will depend on what is a customary practice where you are buying as well.)

Contingencies (Any obligation the buyer has to complete before they can consummate the transaction. Example: Selling another home before purchasing this one, completing the closing on another one under contract, etc.)

Fixtures and improvements (Defining what they are if any, if any are reserved, etc.)

How the buyer will take title. (I.E. As an individual, Limited Liability Corporation, etc.)

Assessments (These are usually concerning installment agreements related to the property. Example: A municipal assessment to each house on a street to install a city sewer system may charge every house $75 a year for a period of 10 years, etc.)

- Title Insurance

- Closing date

- Disclosures

- Special Conditions

- Special notices to buyer or seller

- Home Owners/Condominium Association Fees

- Addendums

Purchase agreements can also have additional added documents attached to them called 'Addendums'. Addendums are used for addressing individual items, agreements, or terms that are in addition to the Purchase agreement. Here are some examples on how this can used:

A. An addendum might address the fact that you would like 'the appliances, the riding lawn mower, and a paddle boat to remain with the property'.

B. One could also have an addendum to add or remove a buyer from the contract.

C. If one is moving toward a closing, and the an issue with the title comes up, and requires additional time to resolve, both parties might sign an addendum to add to the purchase contract to extend the closing date to a new date, if the one defined in the Purchase Agreement is approaching and it is clear more time will be needed to resolve the title issues.

Disclosures Regarding Known Material Defects or Conditions

'Caveat Emptor' (Latin for: 'Let the buyer beware') has been generally accepted property law doctrine for buying pre-existing homes in the U.S. The exception is in the hiding of material defects, which by law the seller is required to disclose at a minimum in the sellers disclosure statement.

Whether a non-material defect requires a disclosure depends on the state law governing the property location. Disclosures are specialized forms filled out by the seller that pertain to known material defects, and sometime non-material defect that the seller knows about the property.

There can be many different disclosures, depending on what is customary in the state you are buying or selling a residential property in. Here is a short list of the most common ones:

Sellers Disclosure Statement: Covers a checklist and answers to questions about the various overall condition of the property for review by the buyer. Forty-Seven States require a written seller's disclosure of some kind in the transfer of ownership of residential property, with the exclusion of foreclosures where the seller is the bank and will not know the condition of the property. Three States (Wyoming, Alabama and West Virginia) as of this writing do not require a written seller's disclosure statement.

Here are some of the common items found in a Sellers Disclosure statement. This is by no means a complete list:

- Age of shingles and other roof components.

- Known leaks in the roof or foundation.

- The presence or existence of water in the basement or crawl space.

- The presence of mold or mildew.

- Infestations of wood destroying insects.

- Problems with the sewer lines or septic systems.

- The existence of a well, condition and when the water was last tested.

- Types of insulation used in the home.

- Proximity of farmland or commercial property.

- Paid or unpaid assessments (Example: A city assessment to install sidewalks or street lights in the neighborhood.)

- Existence and location of underground fuel storage tanks.

- Functioning plumbing, electrical and gas lines.

- Condition and operational status of the HVAC systems.

- Operational status, existence and condition of a fireplace or wood burning stove.

- How long they have owned the home.

- How long they have lived in the home.

- Pending litigation or arbitration on the property

- Existence or condition of a pool, spa or hot tub.

- Existence or condition of a sprinkler system.

- Existence or condition of smoke detectors, fire alarms and security systems.

- The presence of radon gas on the property.

- The existence and related fees (if any) of a homeowners association.

Lead Based Paint Disclosure: This is a Federal requirement in the sale of all residential real estate in the country, and discloses to the buyer the known or unknown presence of lead based paint on the property by the seller, and gives the buyer an opportunity based on what is disclosed to decide whether they choose to have test performed for lead based paint on the home. Homes built before 1978 are subject to the presence of lead based paint, as this was the primary type of paint used in all residential housing prior to that date. It is the buyer's decision to test for it or not.

Mold Disclosure: This is a disclosure of the known or unknown existence of harmful mold on the property by the seller to the buyer.

Agency Disclosure: This is a disclosure your Realtor will often have you sign, which defines in what capacity they are working with you.

Flight Path Disclosure: Around certain military bases in the country, a flight path disclosure is required to notify the buyer where the property is located in relationship to the air base approach. This can also be found sometimes for properties located near certain commercial airports.

Chinese Drywall Disclosure: In the early 2000's drywall products were imported from China that were later determined to contain hazardous materials and create corrosive damage to plumbing and duct systems, as well as introduce toxic poisons into the breathing space of where it was used. Some States like California are now beginning to require additional inspections and disclosures on newly constructed homes to determine if it exists.

Disclosures Regarding Non-Material Defects or Conditions

Known material defects are common to be required by law for a seller to disclose, and some of those disclosures are listed above. However what about non-material defects?

A non-material defect is usually something related to the home that may not be readily observable with the property, but may impact the value of the home. Certain States require disclosure of non-material defects, and some do not. Here are some examples:

- Illinois, Idaho, Mississippi, New Hampshire, Oklahoma and Oregon require disclosure of the past presence of drug manufacturing or a meth lab in the home.

- Louisiana requires disclosure if the home has been exposed to crystal meth under its list of material hazards, along with electromagnetic fields and contaminated soil.

- California and Oregon require the specific disclosure of earthquake zones.

- California has a disclosure about homes on a golf course, that golf balls might break windows. This stems from a court case where a lady sued because she bought a home on a golf course, and someone broke her window with a golf ball.

- Florida has the requirement of disclosure of a known protected animal species if they are found on the property. (For example: The Gopher Tortoise in Florida is a threatened species, and its burrows are protected by State law.)

- Alaska requires disclosure of soil stability, including problems caused by settling, slippage, sliding or heaving.

- New Mexico and Colorado requires disclosure of the presence of abandoned mine shafts or tunnels on the property.

- Washington requires disclosure of the presence of radio towers in the vicinity that can interfere with telephone communications.

- Alaska also requires a noise disclosure from airplanes, trains, dogs, traffic, race tracks and neighbors.

- Colorado has a disclosure for the presence of noxious weeds on a property.

When one is selling or buying a home with a Land Contract, and perhaps working with a private individual, it is important to investigate what the required disclosures are in your State.

Sometimes pre-packaged Land Contract form kits one buys on the internet may not be inclusive of the local State, County or even City requirements for where you are buying. Be sure to check with professionals in your area, or call the State directly to verify you have met all the requirements.

For more information on online resources for real estate contracts, go to the Useful Links section at the end of this book.

Chapter Eight

Stigmatized Property

కావ్యా

Sometimes a property can become stigmatized from something that happened there, on the grounds or around it. If a murder or suicide occurred on the property for example, it may impact the desirability of a buyer to purchase it. This impact on desirability, although not a material defect, can lower the property's value.

Sometimes this stigma can be an investor's advantage if they do not have concerns about the history of the home. One can always remodel, and modify a home as needed to make the property desirable again. At some point, as time passes the home can actually turn the corner from being stigmatized to becoming a talking point of history.

Some historical examples are as follows:

1) Months before her murder on June 12, 1994, Nicole Brown Simpson's Condominium containing 3400 square feet of living space was purchased at a sales price of $652,000. After the incident, the

home sat vacant. The home, although comparable in every way to the surrounding community eventually sold after sitting on the market two years for a significantly lower price due to the stigma associated with the property.

2) The Bungalow home Sharon Tate was killed in, in Benedict Canyon, California by the followers of Charles Manson was so stigmatized by the horrible crimes it remained unsold for many years. It eventually was torn down due to the undesirable stigma associated with the home.

3) The home where the six year old JonBenet Ramsey was found murdered in 1996 was also stigmatized. The Boulder, Colorado residence stayed on the market for quite some time, and eventually sold at a loss due to the stigma attached to the property.

4) The famous house in which the film the 'Amityville Horror' was based was stigmatized for years. Since the film was released, the home was renovated. To prevent drive by traffic through the neighborhood, the famous quarter round windows were removed by the new owners. Also they changed the address to keep disturbances down in the neighborhood from sightseers. In May 2010 the home was placed on the market for a list price of $1.15 Million, and eventually

sold for $950,000 in August to a local
resident.

In the process of buying or selling real estate,
should you hear a rumor about a home that may reflect a
stigma attached to it, the National Association of Realtors
recommends the following approach:

A. Determine if the stigma is truthful.

B. Check State law on required disclosure.

C. Determine if the stigma will change the price,
value or buyers willingness to purchase.

D. Discuss disclosure with the seller.

E. Disclose stigmas determined to be factual.

Not every state has requirements for disclosure of
stigmas associated with a property, as it is largely
considered a non-material defect. Many States require
that the buyer inquire about it first in writing to the seller
before a disclosure is required. The following are some
examples of various states and their disclosure
requirements concerning stigmatized property. This is by
no mean a complete list, and presented here for the sake
of example:

- In Connecticut, Delaware, Georgia, New
  Hampshire, North Dakota and Oklahoma
  sellers are required to disclose the prior
  occurrence or a murder, suicide, felony or
  other crime on a property only if the buyer
  asks directly.

- Alaska requires the seller disclose the
  existence of human burial sites on the

property, as well as any murder or suicide within the preceding three years.

- Texas requires the disclosure of a death from suicide, murder, natural causes or accident on the property.

- California requires the disclosure of a death, suicide or murder on the premises within three years.

- South Dakota requires disclosure of a murder or suicide within the prior 12 months.

- Hawaii requires the disclosure of the existence of ghosts, murders, suicides or other crimes.

- Arizona requires the disclosure of the presence of ghosts or known existence of a haunting in a home.

- Minnesota requires disclosure of the presence of human remains, burials or cemeteries on the property.

Non-material defects and stigmas are sometimes covered by a broader approach with certain States. Kansas for example has a simple one line questions for sellers that reads: "Are you aware of any other facts, conditions or circumstances, on or off-site, which can affect the value, beneficial use, or desirability of the property?" and leaves the disclosure in the hands of the seller. Massachusetts also has a similar space provided.

Some Sellers Disclosure statements in States like Georgia allow spaces on the disclosure form for the seller to write in 'Additional Explanations or Disclosures' where non-material defects can be disclosed as the seller deems necessary. Oklahoma allows for additional pages to be added and requires they be attached and this is made known directly above the location for buyer and sellers signatures.

The existence of sex offenders in the neighborhood can also add stigma to a home, although it is also considered a non-material defect. Some States like Virginia and Minnesota make known the contact information for the State sex offender registry on the Sellers Disclosure form for buyers to check themselves. In most States it is the buyer's responsibility to investigate this on their own.

When one is selling or buying a home with a Land Contract, and perhaps working with a private individual, it is important to investigate what the required disclosures are in your State. Sometimes pre-packaged Land Contract form kits one buys on the internet may not be inclusive of the local State, County or even City requirements for where you are buying. Be sure to check with professionals in your area, or call the State directly to verify you have met all the requirements.

Chapter Nine

Buyers Points to Consider

ॐॐ

In a Land Contract, there are specifics that the buyers should look out for and expect. This list is by no means all encompassing, but it covers some key basics:

1) You should save some money, and realize that in a majority of cases involving a Land Contract agreement, you will need a down payment of some kind to offer the seller. Be cautious of any deals that do not require a down payment, as it may be too good to be true. The seller might be offering the teaser of 'no money down' to conceal some other defect in the property, title or problem with location as an example. See later chapter concerning fraud for examples on this. This is why it is always important to have some experienced professional representation reviewing the proposal along with you, such as an Attorney, Title Insurance Representative or Realtor.

2) One should make sure that the payments are under what you can afford. Be sure to factor in

taxes and insurance, set asides for home improvements as well as adjustments for increases in these over time. As the buyer, these now become your responsibility, and most land contracts require that you present proof to the seller of taxes and insurance premiums being paid at the minimum on an annual basis, or this could place you in default on the Land Contract.

3) Make sure the seller records the Land Contract at the Register of Deeds, or local Recording entity as required by your County or State. One can also have a 'Memorandum of Land Contract' recorded that is a simple one page document that states to one and all doing any future title searches on the property that a Land Contract does exist, and it defines the parties, dates it was executed, sales price, etc. Why should you do this? Because if either the Land Contract or Memorandum is recorded, you can demonstrate more easily an ownership interest in the property and can more easily defend your proof of title to the property should something happen to the seller during your contract period. Recording a Land Contract or Memorandum will also prevent the seller from subsequently taking out a mortgage on the property without your knowledge. It also may allow one to qualify for certain tax benefits in your State if it is your principle residence.

4) Have an experienced Realtor or Attorney help you with the transaction, even if you pay them directly. Professionals can make sure the

contract and purchase is done correctly in accordance with your State requirements. They can also connect you with local professionals such as title companies, inspectors, and contractors that can assist you. Many locations, for example, require passing a well and septic inspection before transfer of ownership. In addition, some properties may require structural inspections, or you may want to have a specific area of the house looked at by a contractor. (I.e. furnace inspection, roof inspection, etc.)

5) Pay for and obtain a title insurance policy before you sign for any property on a Land Contract. This insures that the seller has a right to in fact sell you the property, and there are no liens, mortgages, etc. on the title. They can also make sure the deed is properly recorded, as well as any homestead tax exemption paperwork that might be available to you in your County or State.

6) Include in your monthly budget money to set aside in a reserve account to cover future repairs and maintenance should they be needed on the property. Neglect of property maintenance or failure to remedy serious repairs can place you in default in most Land Contracts, and this can prove cost prohibitive to resolve if the funds are not immediately available.

7) If you sublet any portion of the property, be it a room, garage or any other portion of the home in part or in whole, advise your tenant to

secure rental insurance. Homeowners property insurance will not usually cover a rental.

8) Buying a home is an investment in your future. If you have to repair credit, be sure to have a sound plan in place to get your financial house in order in the future before committing to a Land Contract agreement. As stated throughout this book, most Land Contracts have a balloon payment. This will require a lump sum settlement when it arrives. This means you either have to have the cash available, or a certainty that you can qualify for a loan. Be sure to do your homework before you commit, to make certain you will be able to make this happen. Otherwise, you could lose your investment.

Chapter Ten

Sellers Points to Consider

ぺ◌◦ふ

When one is selling a home on Land Contract, one is entrusting a valuable asset to another individual or individuals when extending them credit. The following listed points are for sellers to be mindful of and should consider as important:

1) Do a full application and review on any prospective buyer. As someone who is offering a form of seller-financing, you have a right to require they present credit reports, income and financial statements, and verify employment. Also check public records for judgments, child support garnishments, criminal history, etc. A prospective applicant can 'look good on paper', and present a good income source, but public records such as garnishments and child support can give a much clearer picture of how much they are taking home in actual pay each month. Examining how frequently an applicant has moved in recent history, will also offer insight into their stability.

2) Be cautious of applicants without income.
Further, if their source of income is a form of
government subsidy such as social security,
workman's comp, unemployment, insurance
settlement, child support, etc. Most of these
types of income sources have future limitations
and may expire without renewal. You will
want to have them provide proof of the length
of time of the payments they are to receive, and
make sure there is evidence that this income
will carry through the length of the contract.
You will also want to see a plan from buyers,
despite all good intentions, on how they intend
to address the balloon payment in the future.
Most conventional loans will be difficult to
obtain with low or unstable income. Also if
they must repair credit scores while waiting
for the balloon, you may want to see that plan
as well.

3) Require a down payment. The more sizable
the better, as this makes for a more
responsible homeowner who is more likely to
take care of the property and be motivated to
make his or her payments on time so they do
not lose their investment. It is the age old
adage of making sure someone has 'Skin in the
Game' to increase confidence they will stick
through to the end of the agreement. 10% to
20% is an average down payment standard for
most Land Contracts.

4) Require a full year's home owners insurance
paid and presented, before any contract is
signed. Require that they present proof of
payment of annual insurance and property

taxes every year, and make sure this is defined as constituting a condition of default in the land contract itself. In some cases a bi-annual or quarterly proof may be necessary, depending on the State you are in and the amount of taxes and insurance required on the home. You may also consider arranging for an independent company to manage and maintain the escrow account for you if these are available in your area.

5) Record the land contract and make sure the tax bills are sent to and paid by the buyer. Payment history can be checked online, and this should be done annually or semi-annually depending on the billing cycle of the tax collection department.

6) Make sure all utilities are transferred into the purchasers name before you turn over the keys. Failing to do this can make it difficult to collect later, and leave you liable for the bills with the utility company. If you live in a colder climate, it might not be unreasonable to require that utilities be maintained as a term of the land contract. Frozen pipes can create a lot of damage in a home when someone neglects their heating bill.

7) Make sure you are listed as the payee on the beneficiary on the homeowners insurance in the event of a total loss due to fire or other natural disaster. Keep a copy in your files, and periodically call the insurance company to verify you are still listed as such, or require notification in writing should this ever change.

Most insurance providers provide for notification, so be sure this is in place. Some sellers in certain circumstances may also take out a life insurance policy on the purchaser payable to the seller to pay off the note in the event that the purchaser dies to cover the balance of the contract as an extra measure of security.

8) Remember to leave the buyers to their own quiet enjoyment of the property. Just because you have a Land Contract with them does not mean you can drop by unannounced. Always send advance notice either by means of phone or mail for any planned visits. Some State laws require this as a procedure as well.

Chapter Eleven

Seven Steps in the Land Contract Quest

෨෬෨

"Hello, is this Michael?"

"Yes it is. How can I help you?"

"I just read your article on land contract homes in my area, and I want to set up a time tomorrow to go looking at some with you."

"So you read the article?"

"Yes, and I would like to go look at some."

"Okay...Pardon me for saying so, but it does not appear that you read the article I wrote in full. It explains in that article that Land Contract homes are not very commonly available. In actual fact they are approximately available about 1 - 2% of the time in the entire market of available homes. However, if you have money to put down, usually in the range of $5000 to $10,000 and can fill out a credit application, I can do some research and try to find a seller who is willing to do one..."

"Well, that is just it. I have the money, but not the credit."

"Do you know what your credit score is?"

"I was told it was 625, and that was not high enough for my bank to loan me the money."

"Did you only check with your bank?"

"Yes"

"Would you consider allowing me to have mortgage brokers look at your credit, and income, and see if they can qualify you for a government loan program such as FHA or USDA Rural Development. If they cannot, they perhaps they can recommend a short term credit repair program to try to improve your score, and clean up your credit enough to get you qualified for a loan?"

"Wow! You can do that?"

"Yes, I can. It would perhaps open up a few new doors for you in terms of options."

"Well, it is important to me to get into a home by December."

"That is highly possible. Let me have a lender call you and do an interview and see where we stand. Then once that road is explored, then, we can explore the option of a Land Contract purchase if needed."

"Thank you so much!"

For twenty years I have had an interest in Real Estate from many perspectives. I have been an enthusiastic property investor, homeowner and also a licensed Realtor. I have bought and sold properties, and have been involved in the sale of real estate in various transactions over the years in Georgia, Michigan, Indiana, Arizona, North Carolina and Florida.

In all this time, I have seen and experienced many hurdles one has to go through in order to buy or sell Real Estate, whether Commercial, Agricultural or Residential. However, one of the most interesting topics that I have encountered in all of those years is the attraction to a form of financing called a 'Land Contract'.

Years before I truly understood the subject as I do as a Realtor, I had many friends tell me 'Try to get a Land Contract on a home, if possible; it is so much easier'. When I bought my home in Michigan in 2001, I asked a few Realtors 'Can you show me homes offering Land Contract terms?' only to be told 'Land Contracts are not much done around here...' or some other canned answer. When I found the home I eventually purchased, which was for sale by owner, I even asked the seller if they would accept a Land Contract, and they said 'yes' and we did explore the option. I later went the route of a mortgage instead, which I determined at the time to be the better solution.

However, the subject of seller financing through a privately held note fascinated me. When I became a licensed Realtor in later years, I was awestruck by the number of inquiries I received each week from prospective buyers who had also been given similar advice about Land Contracts. In many cases, they really did not know what they were. In some cases, they were quite informed, and swore by the method as the best for them.

As a matter of importance, I decided that I better know more about this subject. I began to speak to my broker, colleagues, title company (Companies involved in examining and insuring title claims for real estate, on behalf of its customers) professionals, and many other people I interacted with in the course of selling homes. I also sought out material on the subject, where available around the internet. I soon discovered that there really was not any single book written on the topic specifically, but mainly a lot of word of mouth and this ever persistent 'Urban Legend' ideal that had evolved over the years to represent as a it being 'Just as easy as renting, but your buy the home instead'. However far from the truth that was, I was surprised on how many believed it to be gospel.

I decided to start formulating information for buyers on the subject. I even wrote a pamphlet for buyers to mail to them, hoping this would help give them a better understanding of the subject. As the blogosphere began to develop in the mid 2000's, I expanded my online education to writing a blog on Real Estate. As years followed, I wrote many blogs. In this time, I have written several blog articles talking about how Land Contracts commonly work. I wrote these articles mainly as educational pieces to better inform readers on the subject, and to try to shine the light of truth on this 'Urban Legend' misinformation of the subject. It was my intention initially to present information in hopes to create a better educated caller when they do call.

However, what seems to be a typical occurrence, the reader skims the material written, and says "This guy knows about Land Contact homes, so he must have a lot of them, so I will just call him..." Thus they call me directly. It does not matter to them that they have not read the article.

I do not mind it particularly, as I am a Realtor, and I enjoy helping people. In many cases an extensive overhaul of their financial situation is needed to help them cross that final bridge and become a homeowner, but some are not committed to taking the journey necessary to resolve their financial instability.

As a licensed Realtor in Michigan I can tell you that the following two examples that I included in this chapter are common calls. Over the years I have received many such calls, and so have many of my colleagues. In first example I give, as a matter of fact, is essentially the exact outline of a call I received just a few days ago as I write this.

Allow me to offer some insight into what happened in the first example given at the start of this chapter. This woman went to her bank, which had limited loan programs, and the loan officer, instead of letting her know that there were other loans that exist in the market that she could likely qualify for, placed her on a program to 'wait and let's see what her score looks like in a few months...'

If you were to go buy any other product in the market, and not find what you wanted at one location, would you give up? Would you take the word of the employee who works there when they say 'Sorry, but we do not have your shoe size, and it is unlikely that you will find any at our competitors, so why don't we just wait and see if your foot changes size in the next few months?'

Sounds absurd, doesn't it? However that is exactly what happens when shopping for a mortgage. You must realize that one location may not have all the answers, and they may also have an interest only in selling you their products.

The truth is that this buyer was grossly misinformed that other programs exist. Therefore this was a vital step skipped in the process for her. All she had explored were the typical conventional loans offered by that particular banking institution. Her bank probably had some internal policy that they never refer to another lending institution, for fear of losing business, so the prospective buyer was given the canned answer of 'Oh, there are no other options than to wait' or the sometimes more common misdirection of 'You will get the same answer from other lenders with that credit score, so let's wait a few months and see if it improves...'

As a buyer you must explore beyond your own personal banking institution for a loan. When they come looking for a Land Contract home, they are seeking this approach because they think they have explored all their options, when in fact they have not. They are then grasping for the brass ring of the Urban Legend as the last effort of hope, when in fact many times they did not know the flame was not extinguished.

The truth is that if one has bad credit, or a low credit score, this score will need to be improved either now or within 2 years, even with a Land Contract home purchase, as a typical Land Contract or Contract for Deed arrangement will have a balloon payment around the 2 year mark on residential real estate.

This means you will need to:

A. Get your credit score improved in that time in order to qualify for a loan from a conventional source.

B. Or pay off the note with a lump sum cash.

C. Or renegotiate with the seller (if they are willing) on a new contact term.

So it is a good idea to explore a credit repair program first, before deciding on an option for a Land Contact.

The proper sequence would be:

1) Check several independent sources for a loan, and see if the story is the same with the conditions of obtaining a loan.

2) Find out how extensive a credit repair will be required.

3) Determine if the timeframe is short if it is better to just take the steps necessary to get your credit repaired on a short term, or if it will be a longer term repair, if a Land Contract option with a 2 year balloon will allow you enough time to fix any credit issues you might have to address in that time.

The second and far too typical phone call I receive commonly goes something like this:

"Hello! I saw your article online about land contract. I want to get a home with one, and seeing that you wrote about it, I thought I would give you a call."

"Okay, great. So you read my article, and you understand that you need three things: a down payment of usually 10% to 20% down, and be able to fill out a credit application, demonstrate income and be in a position to qualify for a loan in 1-3 years depending on your credit situation and what terms we negotiate with the sellers?"

"Oh... I don't have any money, and only disability income (no job) and my credit is horrible..."

Repairing your Credit:

This profile of a wishful buyer is not going to be a candidate for a Land Contract. They have no income beyond a low disability check, no down payment, and are going to be in no financial position to repair their credit in 2 years time if their credit damage requires settling old debts, etc.

Unfortunately there are many calls in this category, more so than the first example above. However, there is still hope for them as well. The steps required to accomplish their goal of homeownership requires a more expanded approach to becoming a homeowner, addressing fundamentals in their life. However daunting this may seem, it is still possible to be done.

I have written a proven basic seven step program to help anyone overcome their financial situation.

The Seven Steps:

1) What would be the first thing you would need to do personally? Change your mind. By this I mean change the fundamental way you look at life; starting with yourself. How can you do this? I cannot provide you with the magic words to change your thinking for you, nor can anyone else. I suggest you do this only to make

yourself more eligible to become a homeowner. Change your mind about how you have decided to live your life. The Philosopher Siddhartha Gautama, also known as Buddha once said 'He is able who thinks he is able'. As stated earlier, homeownership requires commitment. Are you in anyway prepared to embark? This may require some 'soul' searching, but I recommend that you have this answer before you start looking into buying your home. Be willing to change your mind about how you have done things until now, and be willing to examine new ideas.

2) Decide that you are able to change your condition, and look for a solution. Answers do not happen overnight, but they do happen quicker if you do step #1 and decide you are able to do something about it. Are you prepared to look for answers? Start by learning from others who have done what you want to do. Read books, talk to successful people, open yourself to new ideas and change methods and patterns of the things in your life that have gotten you where you are now, and point them in a new direction of where you want to go. Abraham Lincoln lost 8 elections (Including twice running for U. S. Congress, and twice for the U. S. Senate), and failed twice in business before he was elected President of the United States. He was quoted once as saying: "Always bear in mind that your own resolution to succeed is more important than any other."

3) Change your lifestyle and the basis of which you operate currently. For Example: If your

day consists of staying up late at night, watching TV, and sleeping in until noon on weekends... Is this getting you where you want to be? Really take an honest look at it. You might make the decision to turn the TV off entirely for a month, and spend your time reading, for example. Libraries are free, and a great place to start. Seek out new ideas on how you can engage yourself in life. Is there something that you have always wanted to do? Try making a list! There are even online courses you can take, and training that you can do to start a new career. With the Internet connected world we live in today, there are endless possibilities if one just starts to look.

4) Charles Dickens once wrote: "I never could have done what I have done without the habits of punctuality, order, and diligence, without the determination to concentrate myself on one subject at a time." His life's work included the timeless novels 'David Copperfield', 'Great Expectations', 'A Tale of Two Cities', 'Oliver Twist', 'A Christmas Carol' and numerous other novels and short stories.

5) The early days of his life in 1824 saw his own father sent to prison for debt when he was twelve years old. He had to leave school to work at a rat infested factory for six shillings a week to help support his family as one of eight siblings. Certainly this is an obstacle, hardship and reality we do not have to face in modern times. It is worthwhile to consider such historical figures of the past to realize that no matter how hard one's own circumstances may

seem at present, someone else experienced the same hardships or had it much worse. If they can succeed, you can to.

6) Make your own money. Receiving a benefit from the government is sometimes necessary for someone for a short term, but if you make it your only source of income for the long term, you are capped at a low ceiling which will prevent you from demonstrating income sufficient to purchase a home. So really reflect on the first 3 steps above, and do something to create a situation where you are making your own money, and supporting your own cost of living under your own steam.

7) Make more money. Too many times people getting rejected on a loan or line of credit are told something like this. However, without these 4 previously mentions steps being done, it's hard to accomplish this. Making more money is a necessity if you are going to clean up damaged credit. Sometimes old debts need to be settled, or have a payment arrangement made. This requires money. The only way to get it is to do more of the same that you worked out as independent income for yourself in the prior steps mentioned here.

8) Save money, and stabilize your income. Lenders lending money, be it an independent bank or a mortgage company always want to see consistent stability in a person's income. Usually they want to see at least 2 years income. Sometimes longer is required if you

are self employed. Cash reserves in terms of savings are also things they look for.

9) Use this new vehicle of income and stability you have created for you and settle any old debts and fully repair your credit. Most bad credit situations can be completely overhauled within a two year period with some aggressive debt negotiating and settling of old debts. I will cover more about this in a later chapter on credit repair.

Chapter Twelve

Profiles of Property Ideal for the Land Contract Solution

છેઅ

Sometimes the extended wait for a little credit repair to qualify for a loan is safer and less expensive in the long run than being under represented in a land contract. I have done many land contract transactions, but they all had to conform to the certain conditions as defined in this book to make them worthwhile for both parties. There have been cases where I have recommended against a Land Contract if it did not conform to the guidelines that I defined in earlier chapters.

With a market environment containing a lot of foreclosures that have been severely discounted, often it is a better route to overcome whatever barriers needed to become approved for a loan in the long run. A majority of banks selling properties in foreclosure do not accept Land Contract terms for resale. For that reason, I will cover a general outline of some credit repair basics in the next chapter.

If your credit is hopelessly shot, seek to gain a better understanding of market conditions, and how such a deal can be put together when you are in the situation of having no credit and little or no reserve funds but a good income.

With so many homes having been sold on mortgages in the last two decades, few homeowners today own their home free and clear. According the U.S. Census Bureau in 2008, 51 Million households had a mortgage, and 24 Million homes were owned free and clear. Another 37 Million reported that they rented the home they lived in. This places a homeowner that owns their home free and clear to represent approximately one out of every five or six homes on a national level.

Homeowners who do own their homes free and clear would often be in a better condition to sell their home to a buyer with financing, rather than carry a note on a Land Contract. Often they need to sell, and cash out in order to purchase elsewhere. However, receiving a sizable down payment from a Land Contract can often be a good resource on a down payment on a new home, so this can be a win-win situation.

Foreclosed homes are owned by large banks looking to sell and liquidate, and will not consider a land contract as an option to sell. Instead, if the home does not sell, they will simply just lower the price and continue to do so until a cash buyer or financed buyer comes along to buy it. This eliminates any possibility of a land contract being an option in those cases. However, I have known some small local banks and credit unions to be open to the proposal of a Land Contract on homes they are holding as foreclosures, and are having difficulty selling by conventional means.

The buyers in these cases submitted a financial application along with a business plan and plan for credit repair within a time frame the sellers were comfortable with, and they were able to get it approved through the bank review boards. So there are exceptions to every rule.

Large banks (i.e. Chase, Wells Fargo, Bank of America, etc.) selling foreclosures as a rule will not consider a land contract. They sell their property through independent 'Asset management' companies with specific instructions for cash liquidation methods only.

This limits them to cash and new mortgage sales for those homes. As stated before, many of the individual sellers on the market have mortgages on their homes, so finding a seller who owns a home free and clear of any mortgages is unusual.

So what type of seller will sell on a land contract in these market conditions you might ask? The seller of a very specific type of property...

There is an outline of a type of property that would make an ideal property to put a deal together on a land contract.

Here is what to look for in a property as a buyer to open the door of opportunity for you:

1) As stated before, a seller who owns a property free and clear.

2) A seller with a mortgage that has been paid down, and does not have a 'due on sale' clause.

3) A property that has not sold, and has a peculiar oddity about it. An odd floor plan, unusual lot

shape, high traffic location or incline that would not appeal to an average buyer who is qualified and has many others to choose from.

4) A home in an area where no other homes are selling.

5) A location which has an unappealing external element, such as a noisy highway, airport, or adjacent industrial property.

6) A home requiring extensive repairs. It should be one requiring work that you have skills, resources and are capable of doing, and at the same time be able to afford your Land Contract, tax and insurance payments.

7) Stigmatized properties as described in the earlier chapter on disclosures.

8) Properties with any other form of non-material defect as defined earlier.

In short, you need to change your entire thinking pattern on what type of home you need to look for if you are going to strictly seek out a land contract deal. The laws of competition with financed buyers, cash buyers, etc. will rule out all the other highly desirable property such as ones with a great view, acreage, good conditions or quiet rural setting. These types of homes are at the top of the list for buyers with loans and cash, and if you are trying to compete with them, you will often run into a lot of dead ends and little success.

As a Realtor, I have seen great homes in need of repair, or just is a peculiar location that otherwise were sound homes. They just had something noticeably odd about them that mainstream buyers were turned off by. If the seller were willing, and able to offer a Land Contract, I would often propose that as a sales option, and we would always pull in a Land Contract buyer.

A home with some kind of oddity can often sell for more money for the seller than he or she would normally receive with a buyer with a loan or cash available to them. The buyer on a Land Contract might pay a little more, but the trade off is for favorable terms and flexible seller financing that they otherwise would not have been able to qualify for.

So in these kinds of cases, it can be a win-win for both parties. The seller gets to sell a home they have not been able to sell through conventional means, and the buyer gets to buy often more home, just with some sort of oddity, that they would not be able to have gotten into otherwise.

I once had a seller who was an elderly woman living in a nursing home. She needed to sell her house so she could meet the qualifications for her Medicaid, and remain at the center she was at. The trouble was the home was only 550 square feet, having two small bedrooms, only a small basement unusable for living space, etc. The woman had lived in the home with her husband for 50 years, and during that time the surrounding neighborhood had been rebuilt with multi-family housing, so this was impacting the appeal as well.

The family approached me to sell it for them. After several months attempting to find a cash investor to buy the home, I finally was able to sell it to a man who was a disabled veteran looking for a place only for himself alone with no one else. It worked out as a win-win for all involved. This is a good example of a peculiar property, which was hard to sell due to its peculiar size, but it sold within a few weeks of offering it on a Land Contract.

So when hunting for a home that you would like a property owner to sell to you on Land Contract, seek out the 'Ugly Duckling' or 'Island of Misfit Toys' and you will have discovered the proper frame of mind to be successful in your search. Homes that conform to the mainstream demands of the marketplace will have no motivation to be sold other than conventional financing, as there is demand.

So one could surmise that a proper approach to be successful in your search would be to find out what homes are in demand in the area or market, and work backwards in your thinking. Find what the highly demanded 'norm' is and then look for homes outside of the norm. With that approach you will have greater success in finding your prize.

Chapter Thirteen

Prevention of Fraud and Other Snarls

కంళ

When one is covering the subject of Land Contracts, it is necessary to also address the subject of fraud. For every example of fraud given herein, be sure there are a dozen others being invented by criminals as we speak.

To be alert to it, one must have some understanding on what to look for, and how it can happen. I have written this chapter to relay not only an account of some experiences I have come across with land contracts, unscrupulous investment schemes, and the lot. I helped some clients unravel a morass of real estate financial snarls, and essentially take steps to do damage control after they had fallen prey to a massive fraud scheme. I worked with these clients to sell off real estate they had acquired for half of what they paid for long after they had lost a great deal of money, and severely damaged their financial futures.

I will begin by telling you about a series of incidents that occurred in 2006 and 2007. In late 2006 I was given a referral to four separate women that were in deep financial trouble and they needed help in selling some properties. It turns out they were taken in by the same unscrupulous 'business man' who in fact was a "confidence man". He used their good credit, defrauded the banks and overleveraged several 'investment' properties in their name with their consent. Unfortunately for them, he had been quite successful in deceiving them, and preyed on their desire for a quick profit with their retirement funds.

By the time these women sought help from me after they had discovered what this man had tricked them into doing, the damage had been done. They lost several hundred thousand dollars combined in 'investment homes'. Upon discovery of the scheme, as it unfolded when they told me the story, I reported the matter to my Real Estate broker. Together we reported those who perpetrated the scheme to the Federal Bureau of Investigation, who took detailed depositions from all these victims.

These trusting women had been taken in by this 'Investor/Property Manager/ Business man' in 2005 who convinced them to buy houses with mortgages, and have the mortgage bills sent to him, and he would 'manage' the properties for them, pay the bills and send them the profits. He took out first, second and even third mortgages on some of the homes, pulling as much money out of the homes as he could before letting them all lapse into foreclosure.

What in fact happened was that he made a few payments, and then sent the ladies a few checks until they were comfortable. Months went by without him giving them status reports. What he actually did was let all the properties go into default with the mortgage companies after the maximum cash was pulled from each home with each subsequent lien being signed off by the women. In one case, he got a power of attorney from an elderly woman, and took out a home equity line of credit on one of the properties without her knowledge.

He then signed up tenants and 'land contract buyers' in each of the houses, which totaled 15 in all. About 10 of them were sold to 'buyers' who thought they were buying the homes on land contract through the owner. The buyers believed this man to be the owner, and entered into 'hand shake' or loosely written contracts 'avoiding costly attorneys' and they too were taken in the scheme.

The land contract documents even cited the 'Confidence Man' and his company as the owner, and none of the buyers investigated or paid a title company to verify this was accurate. The actual names on each of the deeds were one of these four ladies. The 'Confidence Man' took every dollar he could borrow on the homes, took every down payment he could get from the Land Contract buyers, and grabbed every rental deposit he could and then disappeared.

As stated before, during the purchasing process, none of the buyers on these phony 'Land Contracts' consulted a Realtor, or an attorney, and none of them purchased title insurance, much less pay someone to do a title search for them. All of the buyers gave the Confidence man a sizable down payment, moved in, and started living their lives, making monthly payments. Some made extensive modifications and updates to the property, after all, it was their 'home' or so they thought.

Within six months, all the homes went into foreclosure, and all of these 'buyers' not only lost their money, but some were evicted and all had to go find a new residence and start over. The four women who were the true owners had 15 delinquent mortgages and another 15 or so delinquent second and third mortgages on these homes. All had severe damage to their credit. All the homes were hopelessly over-leveraged, and yet I managed to sell off about half of them as short sales to new buyers.

This took 14 months of negotiating with the banks on their behalf, and I managed to unsnarl one of the mortgages on one of the homes for one of the ladies to retain as a personal residence. She had lost her own home in this mess through over leveraging. The other three became renters, and are still renting to this day as far I know, waiting for the foreclosures to fall off their credit reports in 2017; a very sad epitaph for their previously perfect credit histories, to say the least.

What was the real error? They did not hire their own professional advisors of any kind, and trusted entirely everything to be taken care of by this guy. Had they consulted an attorney, a Realtor or even a Certified Public Accountant, they could have been warned of the fraud. Instead they listened to the hype, and never did their own personal inspection to verify the authenticity of the proposal he was making.

The errors the Land Contract buyers made should be listed here as:

1) They did not use a Realtor.

2) They did not consult an attorney.

3) They did not go through a title company, and obtain title insurance.

The 'Confidence Man', who orchestrated this whole fraud scheme, preyed on victims who believed what was said verbally by him. He was persuasive, and was a smooth high pressure salesman.

The buyers of the land contract homes falling for the 'Too Good to be True' opportunity, and in a condition where they trusted the 'hand shake' style of business proposal the man ran, and did not hire a professional in any capacity to check the authenticity of what was being sold to them.

If they had, they would have discovered the following:

1) He did not have any ownership interest in the property, thus could not sell them the home through land contract or any other terms legally. Nor could his 'company'.

2) There was an existing recorded mortgage on each of these properties, and some were double and triple mortgaged. This would have been easily found by a title company, and would have been a major red flag for any title office agent.

3) There were back taxes owed on some of these homes, and some had extant contractor's liens in place.

4) The real owners had no idea the homes were being offered on land contract, and thought they were being rented.

So consider the above examples a cautionary tale regarding Land Contracts and always consult one or more professionals who are looking out for your interests. I can cite examples of many cases where prospective buyers seeking Land Contracts believed they could not qualify for a loan, when in fact they had never investigated it thoroughly.

Sometimes they were turned down by their local bank that had only one or two specific programs, and never consulted another lender to see if they were shown all the options available. In some cases, they could have spent less money up front and gotten into a more stable transaction if they went the route of financing.

Here are some other examples of instances of fraud and other snarls that I have come across that have occurred in Land Contract arrangements:

The Chain: Someone presenting you a home for sale on a land contract, which has already been land contracted to someone else. Sometimes this can become a chain of land contracts, and if anyone along the line fails to make a payment, the occupant could lose out and be removed from the property as a squatter, or placed in eviction proceedings at the very least with little or no defense if any of the parties on the chain are not located or become missing.

The Too Good to Be True Scheme: Low cost 'too good to be true' Land Contract schemes abound. An investor who is familiar with the system and the courts will buy a home that is barely livable, and sell it on Land Contract to a buyer with a lower than average down payment and monthly payment plan.

Once the buyer moves in they discover huge problems with the house, and spend money on repairs, and fall behind on the payments. The seller follows default proceedings in the District Court, and has the buyers evicted from the property, keeping their down payment, monthly payments, etc. As soon as the buyers are out, they make it barely livable again, and sell it to the next set of unsuspecting buyers, and repeat the process over and over. Protected from landlord tenant laws, because they are not renting the home, the sellers can frequently make a profit on such a scheme over and over again until caught for some other illegal infraction in the community.

The Craigslist/Newspaper Ad scam: A buyer responds to an ad in the newspaper or on craigslist for a Land Contract. The terms sound good, they do a drive-by on the house and it looks great! They go to contact the seller, and discover it is a long distance number or they only provide an email address. The seller is out of the country, and has a story of how they had a job transfer to London, etc. Need to sell their home, the buyer is welcome to go look in the windows, etc.

The house looks great, so the buyer agrees to take it. They are sent some documents, sign them and send money out of the country and are sometimes sent a set of keys. Once they send the money, they never hear form the contact person again.

It is a classic scam. The house often is a vacant property in foreclosure, or an empty vacation rental, etc. It usually occurs with rental scams, but Land Contract ones do occur as well. Buyers should always insist on a face to face transaction, and never get involved with any arrangement to send money out of the country.

Fictional Ownership Sales: A seller sells a buyer a property on a Land Contract. Insists they do the transaction between each other, and save the money on professionals. They particularly do not want to involve a Realtor, Attorney or Title Company. The Land Contract is written, the money is taken, the buyers move in, and after a while start receiving foreclosure notices in the mail for the residence they are living in. This kind of scam takes on many forms.

Criminals get access to homes that are in foreclosure, and get money from the real owner to 'manage' it for them, take it off their hands in some elaborate scheme, save it from foreclosure, etc. They never obtain clear title, and act as a middle man and sell it to some unsuspecting buyer on a Land Contract. The title is not clear, title never passes to the buyer, and the real owner's credit is ruined as in the case example I described earlier in this chapter. The best protection a buyer can have in this is to go through a title company, and pay for title insurance protection, always.

The Vanishing Down Payment: A seller sells the home on a Land Contract. He/she has an existing mortgage, but it is discovered it does not have a 'Due on Sale' Clause. He/she sells the home on Land Contract to a buyer. All parties agree to a price that is more than the balance on the mortgage, including the down payment, so all looks good on paper.

The parties close on the Land Contract, and buyer gives the down payment to the seller. However, the seller never takes the down payment and applies it to the mortgage.

He/she uses the funds for something else. Time passes, and the buyer performs on the Land Contract, and comes to the balloon payment with plans to settle the balance owed with a conventional loan. However it is soon discovered that the balance owing on the mortgage is more than the Land Contract settlement due to the fact that the original down payment was never applied to it.

The seller no longer is in a financial situation to pay the difference. So the buyer becomes a victim of fraud. They can either pay the balance of the loan, or lose the home entirely. It is ultimately a 'lose-lose' proposition for them, or they can take the seller to court and pursue a costly legal battle with an uncertain outcome.

To avoid an outcome like this, the buyer should insist the down payment be made payable with certified funds directly to the mortgage company, and not to the seller.

Chapter Fourteen

Remedies for Default

ॐ∙ॐ

What is Default?

Default is defined as: Failure to fulfill an obligation, especially to repay a loan or appear in a court of law. In a Land Contract, default can be further defined as: Failure to make timely payments, maintain the property, insure or pay the taxes as required.

So what happens when a buyer defaults on a land contract?

Typically a buyer can fix the situation by:

A. Paying and catching up any delinquent payments.

B. Repairing any damage or addressing any neglected maintenance issues.

C. Pay the insurance premiums, making them current.

D. Pay any and all delinquent taxes, making them current.

If these issues are not remedied, then the seller can pursue legal recourse. When a buyer defaults on a land contract, the seller has several traditional remedies in most States:

A. He may sue for the installment payments on the contract which are due, plus interest.

B. He can sue for specific performance on the land contract.

C. He can sue for damages for the breach of the land contract.

D. He can foreclose on the buyer.

E. If the seller desire, they can rescind the contract by taking action on the 'forfeiture' clause in the Land Contract.

Remedies, however, that involve litigation can be slow, expensive and tedious, and therefore are seldom used. The most common remedy is therefore the last one listed above called 'Forfeiture' and the other is 'Foreclosure'.

Forfeiture: Typically is a shorter and less expensive route for the seller to take. However, it may have to be taken several times, as the buyer can often settle the delinquency to satisfy the judicial proceeding, and may go into default again the future where the process will have to be repeated.

Foreclosure: Is usually more costly, and time consuming for the seller, but results in repossession of the property in the end. However, the added time can place the property at risk to vandalism, or expose the property to being sub-leased by the buyer to another party, etc.

For these remedies to be successful, the Land Contract must be a formal contract. A 'Formal Contract' is defined as one that is a written agreement between both parties that is sealed and witnessed.

An informal contract is any contract that does not require specific legal requirements to be deemed valid and enforceable. Informal contracts differ from formal contracts in that they do not have to be sealed, written, or witnessed. Informal contracts are commonly referred to as "social contracts." For an informal contract to be regarded as a formal contract and considered valid, it must be written sealed and witnessed.

It is an unfortunate circumstance when a Land Contract goes into default and neither party insisted it be drafted and made into a 'Formal Contract'. Informal contracts in many States are not recognized by the courts, so a seller may run into legal difficulty trying to pursue forfeiture or foreclosure proceedings in their State.

Michigan and Ohio, as an example, provide for both of these remedies for default: Forfeiture and Foreclosure. Both of these States take a similar approach. I suggest researching these two methods for other States online, to see which is the going to be the best resolution for your situation.

Common Sense Resolutions

When a seller is dealing with a buyer occupant that has gone into default on a land contract, it is always best to first try direct one on one communication to resolve the problem for all concerned. In any situation of default, I would always recommend this course of action as a first step prior to pursuing any legal recourse. Using the legal system to resolve a dispute should only be done when all other efforts have failed, as it can be costly and time consuming.

Here are a few suggestions that any seller dealing with default should consider first.

1) Talk to the buyer and find out what is going on. Have they had a change in their life that suddenly makes it impossible to perform on their original agreement? Sometimes you might find that they lost their job, had an accident, had a death in the family, or some other set back that now makes it impossible or a constant struggle to make the payments.

2) Propose a solution from any of the following, or create one of your own that works:

    A. Amend the contract to allow for 2 payments a month (every 2 weeks). Sometimes the lower payment is just what they need to put in some control for the situation, despite it working out the same in the end.

    B. Propose a different day of the month that the payment becomes due. This too can be something you can amend on the agreement.

    C. Help them find a place they can afford, and get them to give you the house back with a mutual release of the contract as long as they give it to you in the same or similar condition that they received it in. Sometimes getting the house back without a fight in court is the best solution in the long run.

D. Give them some moving money, in return for them surrendering the house in a broom clean condition and signing a release of the contract. Why give them moving money? In some cases this is what is needed to get them out peacefully. A fight in court would be far more costly. I will give you an example: I once purchased a house for an investment company. We bought the house from a man losing it to foreclosure. We paid the mortgage company for the balance of the house, knowing that we were inheriting a tenant. The investor did not want the tenant in the house, as the intention was to do a full remodel, and there was no lease agreement.

So rather than fight a costly court battle, we approached the tenant and found out all she wanted was help moving, and some money for a security deposit on a new place. We paid $700 to a new landlord of her choosing, and rented a truck and paid for two employees to be at her disposal and assist her with the move. We got her out for a total expense less than $1200 and she was moved within 5 days of our buying the house. A legal battle would have been far more costly, and it could have taken as much as two months to get her out.

    E. Restructure the amortization schedule to lower the payments, and increase or adjust the time before the balloon. Sometimes this is a good solution, but realize they need to pay the note down enough and qualify for a loan in the end, so make sure it works.

The main point I would tell sellers is that they should always explore a civil face to face resolution that works for all parties before engaging the legal machine. Other professionals might suggest differently, but I have found it to be the case in a majority of the situations that if the occupants are approachable and willing to talk to you, you usually can find a way to resolve the problem amicably. In the case of default, I would much rather get the house back in a livable condition without repairs, and be able to make it available to other buyers quickly rather than be engaging in a costly legal battle. Even if this means paying some out of pocket expenses to do so.

Remember that when a buyer defaults, and has to walk away from the land contract, they lose all of their investment. They are entitled to none of their down payment, or accumulated monthly payment, etc. So the seller never loses. If the buyer just wants out, because they need to get out from under the obligation, make it easy for them to do so and get possession of your property as soon as you can.

Even mortgage companies have begun to wise up to this in the foreclosure turbulence of recent years. Legal battles are costly. Mortgage companies trying to avoid foreclosures followed by the cost of eviction will offer the occupants 'cash for keys'. Their usual procedure is to send in a local Realtor, and have them present a document that if the person will surrender the home in 'broom clean' condition by a certain date (usually 2 weeks) they will give them money to do so. I have seen mortgage companies pay anywhere from $500 to $3000 to get an occupant out rather than have to hire an attorney for eviction. I have personally negotiated a few of these for the banks over the years, and I have always found the occupant relieved to be presented with an amicable way out.

So offer the buyer in default an easy way out and try to get your property back without a legal struggle whenever possible. Always have them sign a release of all rights to the property, a quit claim deed, or whatever instrument is legal in your state to release them from obligation and get them off any document on the title without further financial obligation and make it easy for them to do so. Years of experience has taught me that for the seller, this is the lease costly and less difficult route to follow in the long run.

If you are a buyer reading this, and you are in default, don't just wait for the seller to contact you. Be proactive, and reach out to them. Propose a solution that works for you, and the seller might be more willing to help you. Understand that the seller in a land contract is not a landlord. They are not obligated to return any money to you. However, they can release you from your obligation if you can convince them to do so. Perhaps that might be the best thing for you.

As a buyer, a default on a land contract in most cases will never impact your credit report, as it is typically a private arrangement between individuals unless you force the seller to take you to court and obtain a judgment. So if something unexpected happens in your life that requires you to go into default, be willing to talk to the seller and move on. If you damage the home or require the seller to take you to court, they will often be able to get a judgment against you, and that can go on your credit report. They can also seek garnishment of wages and future tax returns in order to collect judgments.

So it is in your best interest to try to resolve your situation of default peacefully, without the courts. Do not damage or destroy the property, or take other forms of retaliation against the seller. If you have any belief in Karma, these things always find a way back to get you. It is better to walk away swiftly and leave the relationship amicably, and you might find the seller to be a good ally in helping you to get onto a different path if you keep the relationship civil and on friendly terms.

Negotiate towards a mutual release of the land contract, and give them the property back in the same or better condition than you received it. Get a fresh start, and gain wisdom from the experience.

Chapter Fifteen

Credit Repair Tips & Advice

છ૭∝ઉ

How Does One Fix Bad Credit?

There is a great deal of information on credit and credit repair all over the internet these days, and many companies are capitalizing on this as a service industry in itself. However, one can often accomplish a great deal of credit repair oneself, without having to hire a third party.

Here are some basic steps to take if you want to do it yourself:

1) Get a free copy of your credit bureau report. There are three separate credit bureau reporting agencies, and each has a separate report on you. They are *Experian, Equifax* and *TransUnion.* All three are required to give you a free copy of your credit report once a year. I suggest you take on one at a time, and pull one every four months. That way you can cycle through your entire credit history for free once a year. It will take you some time to fix just one of them, so four months is a good time

frame, and three reports multiplied by four months equals one year (3 Reports X 4 Months = 1 Year). The official website to do this online at: **www.Annualcreditreport.com**

2) You can also order these by phone at: 877-322-8228. As a precaution, this website is the one provided for in the Fair Credit Reporting Act, and all others that say they offer the same will charge you money. These reports will not give you your Credit Score, just the report. Do not worry about the score when you are working on repairing your credit initially. You want these reports to find out what is holding the score down, and once you see the report, it will be clear what they are. Use this for clean up purposes, and if you do, then the score will improve and you can check that later on other paid sites around the internet if you choose. One such website is: **www.myFICO.com**

3) One should look for the section on each of the reports that attention is called to in some manner as: 'Adverse Accounts', 'Potentially Negative items', etc. These are the negative items on your credit bureau that are the ugly things that are keeping the score down. Adverse or Negative items can include: Remaining balances on unpaid debts, judgments, public records, delinquent accounts, collections, etc.

4) Select out the negative items that you suspect are inaccurate first, leave the rest for later. If you have documentation proving the incorrect reporting, then write a letter to the credit

bureau that includes your address and social security number, and give the account number and description of the company reporting the negative item. Explain how it is in error, and include a copy of the proof of the mistake, if available. If you lack the evidence immediately, send in the letter anyway, as you can always send the proof later if required.

5) On items that you are not sure about, write a letter challenging it, with the information make it known that it does not match your records. When any dispute of an item on the credit bureau is received, the company reporting the negative credit issue is contacted by the credit bureau. They are then required to show proof of its accuracy within 30 days, or it has to be removed in accordance with the Fair Credit Reporting Act. I once had a credit card company remove an entire reporting history from a friend's bureau that was negative because they had changed their computer system and no longer had the records of the account, and could not verify what they were reporting.

6) It is also recommended that you send in all written disputes certified mail, so that the time it arrives is noted at the bureau. In that way the time it is received can be verified, and the time they take to respond can also be used to your benefit based on the 30 day rule, should further challenges be necessary.

7) If the collection is accurate, contact the company that is reporting the debt and try to

negotiate a settlement. The numbers and contact information are often provided right there in the report. Old debts can many times be negotiated away for much less than what they are seeking to collect, especially very old debt. Make sure that you are given written confirmation for any debts you settle, so that you can send this into the credit bureaus yourself to show it is paid and get it removed from the report.

8) Old debts can fall beyond a statute of limitations, and no longer be collectible. The statute of limitations varies from State to State. Old debts beyond your State's statute of limitations reporting on your credit report should be challenged with the credit bureaus directly and cite the statute of limitations for your State, requesting it be removed. Statutes of limitations for old debt can be researched online by searching "Statute of Limitations for Old Debt" and you will find lists of current laws for each State. Never pay a debt beyond the Statute for the State you live in. Instead, write the credit bureau and report that this is outside the Statute for your State, and demand that it be removed.

9) Get yourself a copy of books on credit repair to further educate yourself on how to accomplish this. Additionally, become familiar with the Fair Credit Reporting Act.

Credit Repair has become a popular subject these days, and there is a lot of information on credit and credit repair to learn online and in books. This should get you started.

Chapter Sixteen

Resources for a Land Contract

৵৽

As you have been reading along through this book, I hope I have given you some useful insight into how to negotiate and structure a Land Contract.

One of the questions I am frequently asked by callers who have read my blogs on the subject is: "Where do I actually find a Land Contract document?"

Well, of course you can go to a real estate attorney and have them draw one up for you. This is a recommended option if you can afford it, but is not one often engaged in when I recommend it, simply because of the costs involved.

So here are a few options to explore in your area to find documents as cost effectively as possible:

Title Companies: You can contact a local Title Company and ask them if they can prepare the docs for you, and what fee they will charge for doing it. Often you will find that this is the most affordable option in your area, so I suggest exploring this one first, as they often have Land Contract documents that have already been review and approved by a Title insurance attorney. Most of the time the fees involved for this are quite reasonable.

Realty Companies: The other option is to hire a local Realty company to prepare the docs for you. You will pay an agent a fee to act as a transaction coordinator in most cases, in which he represents neither party, just oversees the transaction is done correctly. Not all Realty offices can do this, so you will need to inquire if they can.

The Internet: Search online for companies that provide pre-packaged Land Contract documents that you can prepare yourself. Be certain to verify they are legal in your State. You might also want to pay an attorney a flat fee to review them once you have completed them. There are several companies online that offer pre-packaged legal documents, so you should be able to compare rates and packages. Use this book as a guide as well.

Non-Profits: Some organizations such as 'Habitat for Humanity' periodically have homes available for sale on Land Contract on an area. Contact your local Habitat for Humanity in your area to find out.

Final points to remember:

Always make sure whatever contracts or documents you use are legal in the State you are in. In addition, make sure you include any required disclosures.

Always have all parties sign the federally mandated lead based paint disclosure if the house was built before 1978. As a routine, I would recommend that you have this signed even if the home is older than 1978, to make sure that all parties agree on the age. There is a spot on the form provided for homes built after this date, so I suggest it be used and copies kept for both buyer and seller in their files. This provides protection against future claims stating otherwise.

Useful Links & References

కావ

Foreclosure Laws by State:

www.realtytrac.com/foreclosure-laws/foreclosure-laws-comparison

Online Legal Websites for Real Estate forms:

Legal Zoom

www.legalzoom.com

Rocket Lawyer

www.rocketlawyer.com

Law Depot

www.lawdepot.com

Nolo

www.nolo.com

U.S. Legal Forms

www.USLegalForms.com

Legalwiz

www.legalwiz.zom

Resources for Selling a Land Contract:

Amerifunds

www.amerifunds.us

Mortgage Note Buyer US

www.mortgagenotebuyer.us

Cash Flow Connection Pro LLC

www.cashflowconnectionpro.net

Credit Report:

Annual Credit Report

www.annualcreditreport.com

My Fico

www.MyFICO.com

Credit Repair Information:

Federal Trade Commission Consumer Information on Credit Repair: www.consumer.ftc.gov

Reports on Credit Repair: **www.BankRate.com**

Acknowledgments

This book was an inspiration from my experiences and work as a Realtor. To begin, I would like to acknowledge all the members of the Battle Creek Area Association of Realtors who have been such a pleasure to work with, and learn from over the years. They are truly a wonderful group of dedicated people. I especially would like to thank the members of the Board whom I worked so closely with in the last 7 years (from the date of the first time this book was published).

I would like to give a special thank you and acknowledgment to all my colleagues at Troxel Realty LLC. Through the years they have taught me so much, and they have always embraced me as a friend.

I would also like to thank my broker Al Morehart who has always been supportive and a voice of encouragement for all my crazy ideas.

I would like to offer a special 'thank you' all my former clients who have had, and continue to have faith in me as their Realtor.

Finally, I would like to acknowledge the incredible love and support from my wife wonderful Margarita, whom without her help this book would not have been possible. She challenged me to look at details from many viewpoints, and especially that of the reader. Her continuous editing of this material made it possible to mold it into its final form. I could not have completed the project without her

About the Author

Michael Delaware is a Phoenix, Arizona native who now resides in Battle Creek, Michigan with his wife Margarita. He also lived in Georgia for 15 years in the 1980's and 1990's where he owned and operated a stained and beveled glass studio in the Metro-Atlanta area. During those years he was an active volunteer in the community, coordinating annual Arts and Crafts Festivals in the downtown district of Roswell, Georgia. He also participated in Arts & Crafts Shows for over 25 years as a vendor in numerous States. He has been a Michigan resident since 1999.

His other published works include numerous non-fiction books on real estate, sales management, marketing and other self-help topics. He has also published fiction and non-fiction stories for children

As an illustrator and photographer, he has included his works in his own books and blogs. He enjoys hiking and mountain biking in the great outdoors and taking long walks in the woods with his dog.

Currently he is an active Realtor in Michigan and frequent community volunteer. He is a member of the National Association of Realtors, The Council of Residential Specialists, and the Michigan Association of Realtors. He is also an active member of the Battle Creek Area Association of Realtors where he was awarded 'Realtor of the Year' in 2010, and served as Board President in 2011. He founded his own independent publishing company in 2012.

To follow Michael:

www.MichaelDelaware.com

Facebook.com/MichaelDelawareAuthor

Amazon.com/Author/MichaelDelaware

Linkedin.com/in/MichaelDelaware

@MichaelDelaware

Other titles by the author
available as eBooks:

The Art of Sales Management: Lessons Learned on the Fly *(also available in paperback)*

The Art of Sales Management: Revelations of a Goal Maker *(also available in paperback)*

The Art of Sales Management: 75 Training Drills to Build Confidence, Excellence & Teamwork *(also available in paperback)*

Small Business Marketing: An Insider's Collection of Secrets *(also available in paperback)*

Arts & Craft Shows: The Top 10 Mistakes Artist Vendors Make... And How to Avoid Them! *(also available in paperback)*

Arts & Craft Shows: 12 Secrets Every Artist Vendor Should Know *(also available in paperback)*

Inspiration: The Journey of a Lifetime

For Real Estate:

Land Contract Homes for Investors

Going Home... Renting to Home Ownership in 10 Easy Steps

In Children's Fiction:

Scary Elephant Meets the Closet Monster

In Children's Non-Fiction:

My Name is Blue: The Story of a Rescue Dog

More titles will be available in print in late 2013 and in 2014. For a current list of available print books visit:

www.ifandorbutpublishing.com

If you found this book on real estate useful, you might also like these other titles by the same author:

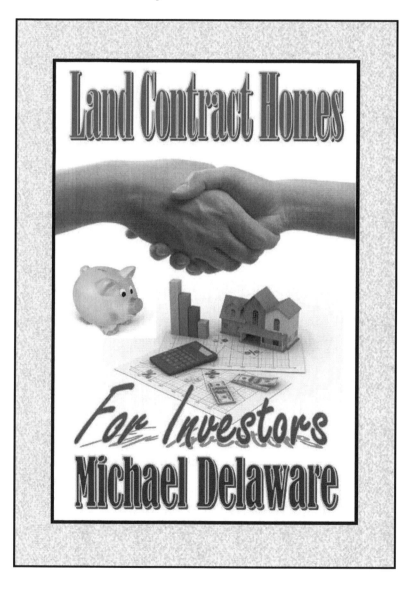

www.IfAndorButPublishing.com

Made in the USA
San Bernardino, CA
20 May 2014